CREATION: OUR WORLDVIEW

DR. GRADY S. McMURTRY

To Sigis,

Grady McMurtry

Col. 1:16

Creation Worldview Ministries
4698 Hall Road
Orlando, Florida 32817
WWW.CREATIONWORLDVIEW.ORG

Also by Dr. Grady S. McMurtry:

Creation Our Foundation

The Redwoods National Park: A Case Study in Legislative Compromise

ISBN: 0-9674006-1-9

1st edition published 1997, 2nd edition 1999, 3rd edition 2000, 4th edition 2003, 5th edition 2008

Dedication

To my daughter Holly, a blessing from the Father above and one of the finest young Christian women I have ever had the privilege to know.

TABLE OF CONTENTS

Content Description and Rationale i

Preface iv

Intellectual Honesty 1

Great Questions in Genesis 1-11, Part 1 19

Great Questions in Genesis 1-11, Part 2 31

The Ark of Noah 37

Job—A Great Book of Scripture and Science 43

Creation in the Psalms 51

The Nine Great "Proofs" for Evolution 63

People Lived to Be 900 Years Old? 101

Environmental Issues and the Christian 109

The Complexity of the Universe 151

Other Reference Sources 161

CONTENT DESCRIPTION AND RATIONALE

This book is designed to be a simple and easy to understand book written at the popular level exploring the biblical teaching on creation—its implications; problems and issues of interpretation: that is, creation vs. evolution; a Christian worldview vs. secular humanism, etc. Major biblical texts involving the topic of creation are included. This book may serve as an introduction to the scientific method and a survey of the basic concepts of the biological, natural and physical sciences with a consideration of related questions which confront the biblical Christian worldview.

1) **A biblical viewpoint of origins (*fiat creation ex nihilo*)** will be studied in both its historical narrative and educational applications. The Book of Genesis indeed conveys the account of the origin of the universe in its entirety in six literal, 24 hour days. Alternative theories of interpretation will be considered and their relative merits will be weighed.

2) **A biblical model of origins** will be compared with the present culturally accepted belief in evolutionary development. The chief proofs for evolution will be considered. It will be demonstrated that they employ both poor science and defective logic.

3) An attempt to lay out a **biblical Christian worldview solidly grounded in biblical creation** will be made. This worldview will be set against alternative worldviews such as secular humanism, Marxism, new age, eastern pantheism, etc.

4) **The historical narrative of the Noahic flood** will be considered from both a biblical and geological perspective. The geologic column as typically presented within an evolution model will be reexamined according to historical geology. Upon completion of this text, you will understand that the millions of years of "geologic time" and a worldwide flood in the days of Noah cannot both be true... and that, at minimum, a biblical perspective of geologic time is, at least, as easy to defend, if not easier, than a compromise viewpoint. Indeed, no compromise is necessary concerning any true scientific statement and Scripture.

TEXT OBJECTIVES

Cognitive

What you should know and understand:

- The Bible presents a clear and defensible model of origins.

- The Bible addresses the age of the earth through its historical narrative.

- The biblical narrative is scientifically vindicable.

- Evolution provides the primary apologetic for many, if not most, ungodly religious and political systems (including liberal Christianity).

Affective

What you should feel and appreciate:

- The Bible is really true, absolutely reliable, and trustworthy.

- The Christian may have confidence in a biblical worldview as a legitimate and effective basis for every discipline.

- Evolutionism is no more than a popular mythology, a fairy tale for adults, set up against the knowledge of God and yields to the light of truth as does any lie. (See Romans 1:25)

- Evolutionists are often deceived by their own schemes and are in need of deliverance the same as any other lost person.

Synthetic

What problems you should be able to solve and what you should be able to do after reading this book:

a. Approach any passage of Scripture as part of one coherent eternal gospel centered in the message of creation: its perfection, fall, and restoration by the Creator (Rev. 14:6-7).

b. Expose the deception inherent in any evolution "proof" strategy.

c. Recognize when problems in behavior, doctrine, or belief can be traced to evolutionism and require creation instruction as a pre-requisite to other ministry being effective.

OTHER REFERENCE MATERIALS

The Holy Bible—NASB or KJV/NKJV or NIV: all referenced Scripture quotes contained in this book are from the NASB unless otherwise noted.

PURPOSE OF THIS TEXT

The purpose of this book is to give you the opportunity to study and increase your knowledge of natural science and how it relates to our Creator. It will help you gain an understanding of the natural world and aid you in establishing a biblical philosophy of science. This book will help you to realize that there are not two different revelations of truth, one natural and the other supernatural.

We do not have a natural revelation which demonstrates that evolution is true and another revelation that states that creation is true. Rather we have one unified revelation which the Apostle Paul summed up when he referred to Jesus Christ as the *Sophia* of God, **the one in whom resides the sum total of all spiritual wisdom and knowledge and the sum total of all natural wisdom and knowledge.** This book will help to develop within you a love for God and God's creation.

PREFACE

For twenty years I was taught to be an Evolutionist. I was an evolutionist, I believed evolution and I taught evolution. During those early years I was not taught with circumspect nor intellectual honesty. I was not taught to think critically nor to correlate data which would contradict the evolutionary philosophies. I was not taught with good educational technique, that being that each student, when confronted with a choice of positions, should be presented with all the evidence for both sides and then be allowed to decide for themselves which choice they will believe.

The fundamental issue concerning the acceptance of creation or evolution is one of origins. Do you accept a natural or supernatural reason for your existence and that of all the things in the universe? Do you accept a purely natural reason or one which is beyond nature? This book will assist you in determining for yourself which worldview you will believe and support.

Dr. Grady S. McMurtry

INTELLECTUAL HONESTY

When approaching the issue of origins, the Theory of Special Creation versus the theories of evolution, it is good to note what evolutionists say about these various theories and to define at least some of the terms used by both sides. The following quotes will help to start this process.

Derek Agar, in a presidential address given to the British Geological Association in 1976, said:

"It must be significant that nearly all of the evolution stories I learned as a student...have now been debunked. Similarly, my own experience of more than 20 years looking for evolution among [early Brachiopods] has proven them equally elusive."

H. S. Lipson, Professor of Physics, University of Manchester, UK, wrote an article in 1980, entitled *A Physicist Looks at Evolution* in which he stated:

> In fact, evolution became in a sense a scientific religion; almost all scientists have accepted it and many are prepared to 'bend' their observations to fit in with it.

In the introduction to the 1971 edition of Charles Darwin's *The Origin of Species*, the editor, L. Harrison Matthews, wrote:

> The fact of evolution is the backbone of biology, and biology is thus in the peculiar position of being a science founded on an unproved theory—is it then a science or a faith? Belief in the theory of evolution is thus exactly parallel to belief in special creation-both are concepts which believers know to be true but neither, up to the present, has been capable of proof.

One of the greatest evolutionists of the Twentieth Century, George

1

Gaylord Simpson, wrote in his book *The History of Life in Evolution After Darwin* (1960),

> Fossils are abundant only from the Cambrian onward...Darwin was aware of this problem, even more striking in his day than in ours, when it is still striking enough...the case at present must remain inexplicable; and may be truly urged as a valid argument against the views here entertained.

Ernst Mayer, ardent evolutionist and head of the science education arm of the National Education Association, wrote a book in 1970 entitled, *Population, Species, and Evolution*. On page 9, he said,

> The study of long-term evolutionary phenomena is the domain of the paleontologist. He investigates rates and trends of evolution in time and is interested in the origin of new classes, phyla, and other higher taxa. Evolution means change and yet it is only the paleontologist among all biologists who can properly study the time dimension. If the fossil record were not available, many evolutionary problems could not be solved; indeed many of them would not even be apparent.

Finally, Charles Darwin wrote in *The Origin of Species*,

> Long before the reader has arrived at this part of my work, a crowd of difficulties will have occurred to him. Some of them are so serious that to this day I can hardly reflect on them without being in some degree staggered....Why if species have descended from other species by fine graduations, do not we everywhere see innumerable transitional forms?...Why then is not every geological formation and every stratum full of such intermediate links? Geology assuredly does not reveal any such finely-graduated organic chain and this perhaps, is the most obvious and serious objection which can be urged against the theory...

As you can see even leading evolutionists question their position knowing that it is "religious" in nature since one must believe in evolution by faith. There are no scientific tests which may be devised in order to prove either position to be true. The Scientific Method requires that testing be done in the present, which yields consistent results and then may be used to prove or disprove a position. If evolution occurred, it occurred in the past and is not available for testing in the present. If creation is true, likewise, it occurred in the past and is no longer available for testing.

The evolutionist proposes that matter, space and time are eternal and that only random chance activities acting uniformly throughout time have caused all of the complexity contained in the universe to evolve into existence. This is a worldview which is based in a naturalistic view in which there is no god, no outside designer nor organizing force. What then is this materialistic view of life called naturalism?

Let us begin to look at what certain words mean that will be used in a discussion of this issue.

What Is Naturalism?

Here are two concise statements which adequately describe what naturalism is all about.

> The raw materials of science are observations of the phenomena of the natural universe. Science — unlike art, religion, and philosophy — is limited to what is observable and measurable and, in this sense, is roughly categorized as materialistic (Helena Curtis and N. Sue Barnes: *Biology*, Worth Publishers, Inc., New York 1989, p.17).

> Naturalism does not explicitly deny the existence of god, but it does deny that a supernatural being could in any way influence natural events, such as evolution, or communicate with natural creatures like ourselves. Scientific naturalism makes the same point by starting with the assumption that science, which studies only the natural, is our only reliable path to knowledge. A god who can never do anything that makes a difference, and of whom we can have no reliable knowledge, is of no importance to us (Phillip Johnson: *Darwin on Trial*,

InterVarsity Press, Downers Grove, Illinois 1991, p. 115).

Creation postulates an initial special creation by God through which all laws, processes and entities of nature were brought into existence as described in the book of Genesis (Scott M. Huse: *The Collapse of Evolution*, Baker Books, Grand Rapids, 1983).

What Is Science?

The words "science" and "knowledge" are interchangeable. The word science simply refers to the entire body of knowledge. They are used interchangeably in different translations of the Bible as well; that is, in 1 Timothy 6:20 (and oppositions of science falsely so called; and oppositions of knowledge falsely so called).

Scientific endeavor consists of what is observable, measurable, experimentally repeatable and predictive. One must be able to do an experiment, and using the same set of circumstances, repeat the experiment coming out with the same results again and again. The consistent results gained should then allow us to predict the future results prior to the conducting of other experiments.

What Is a Hypothesis?

A hypothesis is an unproved theory which is tentatively accepted to explain certain facts. The hypothesis must explain what is known about the phenomenon at the time—it must be consistent with the facts. The hypothesis must be capable of predictions about observations not yet made. It must be capable of being tested and it must have the potential for being proved false.

Once a hypothesis has been formed it must then be testable before it may truly be elevated to the level of a theory. This is why neither Special Creation nor evolutionary theories are truly theories; they are not testable and therefore are really just good working hypotheses. They are called theories simply because of common usage.

What Is a Belief?

A belief is a conviction of the truth of some statement, especially when that statement is based on the examination of evidence. The first question which you must ask when confronted by someone saying that they want you to prove that creation is true is, "What evidence would you accept?" There is no point in sharing evidence, data and information for four hours with someone when what you are talking about would not be accepted by them in the first place.

Consider these simple observations concerning the acceptance (by faith) of those who believe in evolution:

> Our theory of evolution has become, as Popper described, one which cannot be refuted by any possible observations. Every conceivable observation can be fitted into it. It is thus 'outside of empirical science' but not necessarily false. No one can think of ways in which to test it. Ideas, either without basis or based on a few laboratory experiments carried out in extremely simplified systems, have attained currency far beyond their validity. They have become part of an evolutionary dogma accepted by most of us as part of our training (Paul Ehrlich, Professor of Biology, Stanford University, *Evolutionary History and Population Biology. Nature*, vol. 214, April 22, 1967, p. 352).

> At this point, it is necessary to reveal a little inside information about how scientists work, something the textbooks don't usually tell you. The fact is that scientists are not really as objective and dispassionate in their work as they would like you to think. Most scientists first get their ideas about how the world works not through rigorously logical processes, but through hunches and wild guesses. As individuals, they often come to believe something to be true long before they assemble the hard evidence that will convince somebody else that it is. Motivated by faith in his own ideas and a desire for acceptance by his peers, a scientist will labor for years knowing in his heart that his theory is

not correct but devising experiment after experiment whose results he hopes will support his position (Boyce Rensberger, *How the World Works*. William Morrow, New York, 1986, p. 17-18).

We take the side of science in spite of the patent absurdity of some of its constructs, in spite of its failure to fulfill many of its extravagant promises of health and life, in spite of the tolerance of the scientific community for unsubstantiated just-so stories, because we have a prior commitment, a commitment to materialism. It is not that the methods and institutions of science somehow compel us to accept a material explanation of the phenomenal world, but, on the contrary, that we are forced by our *a priori* adherence to material causes to create an apparatus of investigation and a set of concepts that produce material explanations, no matter how counterintuitive, no matter how mystifying to the uninitiated. Moreover, that materialism is an absolute, for we cannot allow a Divine Foot in the door (Richard Lewontin, *Billions and Billions of Demons*, The New York Review, January 9, 1997, p. 31).

What Describes a Scientist?

There are four commonly held beliefs about scientists. These are that they are unbiased, that they are objective, that they are infallible and that they always wear a white lab coat and experiment on rats. However, the truths about scientists are that they are biased, they are not objective, they are human, thus they are fallible and they seldom ever wear a white lab coat (and only a small percentage actually experiment on rats).

First, there is no such thing as true neutrality in human endeavor. It is a laboratory ideal which may only be striven toward. Second, people are likewise unable to be totally objective. Third, no human is perfect and therefore, everyone is fallible. Finally, white lab coats and rats are representative of only a very small part of scientific research.

It can be said then that **EVERYONE** is 100% biased. Review the following chart which is only partially complete but serves to show how everyone is biased.

	Basis	Influence	Bias
Atheist	No God Exists	Can't Consider Creation	100%
Agnostic	Don't Care Can't Know Don't Know	Must Exclude Definite Role of God	100%
Theist	God Deduced	No Absolutes	100%
Revelationist	God Revealed to Man	Absolute Reference Points	100%

Never put scientists on a pedestal and look up at them; they will only fall off and get hurt and you will end up with a crick in your neck.

Since there is no way in which to scientifically prove either position concerning creation or evolution, is there a way in which we can test them? Yes, in science when we cannot test something directly, we test it indirectly. We do this all the time. For example, we make models of airplanes and we test them in wind tunnels before we spend the money to build full-sized planes. This kind of model building goes on all the time.

When it comes to the question of origins we may do the same thing. Let's consider how model building and indirect testing may be used to teach scientifically about origins.

The Two Model Approach to Teaching Origins

How should we approach the teaching of evolution versus creation? The subject of origins is approached at the same time from two different directions. We all approach evolution versus creation with our own preconceived ideas and biases. What we were taught as children plays an important role in how we view these two concepts. What our parents taught us or didn't teach us about God, and what we learned or didn't learn in Church, has a definite impact on our beliefs concerning our acceptance of creation. Also, what we were taught in school and have viewed on television, has influenced us concerning our ideas about evolution.

We also approach evolution versus creation from the standpoint of scientific data. We have literally tons and tons of evidence which may be used to support one side or the other. Many people think that through the use of scientific data, it can be proven that man evolved rather than was created. However, there is strong scientific data to the contrary.

Abrupt Appearance versus Gradual Appearance

When we speak of creation and evolution we could just as easily use the terms *abrupt appearance* and *gradual appearance* to describe the same concepts. We may start our analysis of these two positions by seeing if there is any evidence for gradual appearance.

The following is part of an article which records an answer to a letter written to Dr. Colin Patterson about why he had not put any pictures of transitional fossils, those fossils which would clearly show change from one form to another, in one of his books. The article is not reprinted in full.

Are There Any Transitional Fossils?

None of the five museum officials whom Luther Sunderland interviewed could offer a single example of a transitional series of fossilized organisms that would document the transformation of one basically different type to another.

Dr. Eldridge (Curator of Invertebrate Paleontology at the American Museum) said that the categories of families and above could not be connected, while Dr. Raup (Curator of Geology at the Field Museum of Natural History in Chicago) said that a dozen or so large groups could not be connected with each other. But Dr. Patterson (Senior Paleontologist and editor of a prestigious journal at the British Museum of Natural History) spoke most freely about the absence of transitional forms.

Before interviewing Dr. Patterson, the author read his book, *Evolution*, which he had written for the British Museum of Natural History. In it he had solicited comments from readers about the book's contents. One reader wrote a letter to Dr. Patterson asking why he did not put a single photograph of a transitional fossil in his book. On April 10, 1979, he replied to the author in a most candid letter as follows:

> I fully agree with your comments on the lack of direct illustration of evolutionary transitions in my book. If I knew of any, fossil or living, I would certainly have included them. You suggest that an artist should be used to visualize such transformations, but where would he get the information from? I could not, honestly, provide it, and if I were to leave it to artistic license, would that not mislead the reader?
>
> I wrote the text of my book four years ago. If I were to write it now, I think the book would be rather different. Gradualism is a concept I believe in, not just because of Darwin's authority, but because my understanding of genetics seems to demand it. Yet [Dr. Stephen J.] Gould and the American Museum people are hard to contradict when they say there are no transitional fossils. As a paleontologist myself, I am much occupied with the philosophical problems of identifying ancestral forms in the fossil record. You say that I should at least "show a photo of the fossil from which each type of organism was derived." I will lay it on the line—there is not one such fossil for which one could make a watertight argument. **The reason is that statements about ancestry and descent are not applicable in the fossil record.** Is *Archaeopteryx* the ancestor of all birds? Perhaps yes, perhaps no: there is no way of answering the question. **It is easy enough to make up stories of how one form gave rise to another, and to find reasons why the stages should be favored by natural selection. But such stories are not part of science, for there is no way of putting them to the test.**
>
> So, much as I should like to oblige you by jumping to

the defense of gradualism, and fleshing out the transitions between the major types of animals and plants, I find myself a bit short of the intellectual justification necessary for the job... [bolding added for emphasis] (Ref: Patterson, personal communication. *Documented in Darwin's Enigma*, Luther Sunderland, Master Books, El Cajon, CA 1988, pp. 88-90).

If there are no transitional fossil forms in the fossil record, doesn't that indicate that life forms came into existence whole and complete; that is, abruptly not gradually, and therefore they must have been created?

We may also look at the basic premise of creation and evolution from a purely logical and mathematical methodology. The two views may be summarized in simple formulas which describe the essence of each position.

Formulas Which Describe Evolution and Creation

The evolutionist believes in the eternal state of the material universe because to do otherwise would mean that it all had a beginning; and if it all started abruptly then someone or something had to start it. The whole purpose in believing in evolution is philosophical. The acceptance of evolution allows a person to deny the existence of a creator. If there is no God, then all things are permissible. Evolution could be defined as a religion in which "If it ain't convenient, then it don't fit my religion!"

What is the formula to describe this thought process?

Eternal Matter + Eternal Energy + Eternal Time + Random Chance = Life

a.   A belief that all things started in randomness and chaos

b.   A belief that only long periods of time could explain the complexity which we see around us

What about the creationist? The creationist believes that mass and energy are not eternal. A creationist says that there is a God who made mass and energy; made people out of them; does not require time to do anything; and does nothing by random chance, but is instead purposeful in all things that He does.

There is also a formula which describes this:

Matter (Which is not eternal) + *Energy* (Which is not eternal) + *Intelligence* (An eternal Creator God) = *Life*

 a. A belief in an eternal Designer, Creator, God

 b. A belief that no one creates anything without purpose and meaning

From the Standpoint of Time, What Is Science and What Is Not?

Science can only deal with the present, the here and now. Science may not prove anything in the past beyond the time at which history or scientific research can document specific events. Any other claim is foolish in the extreme. The scientific method of proof is not a historical approach. We cannot go back in time and test anything. It would be pretentious to ask the Creator to create something in a test tube in order for us to prove that He can do it.

How Can We Know Which Is True Scientifically?

How can we know if the theories of evolution or the Theory of Special Creation are true scientifically? We cannot test either one of them directly. Why? Because, none of us were alive at the beginning to bear witness to which theory is true and therefore correct, that is, factual. When we cannot test directly we may only test indirectly. We do this by making models.

Models may be made out of plastic, wood, mathematical equations, computer simulations, chemical formulas or, as in this case, words— a verbal model. Let's look at these two verbal models and their respective sets of predictions. Remember that a hypothesis must be able to adequately predict as well as explain events.

Two Models

The Evolution Model	The Creation Model
Common Ancestry	Abrupt Appearance
1. Continuing Naturalistic Origin	1. Completed Supernatural Origin
2. Net Present Increase in Complexity	2. Net Present Decrease in Complexity
3. A Belief in Uniformitarianism: "The Past is the Key to the Present" Slow and Gradual	3. Belief in Catastrophism: One or More Catastrophies on at Least a Continental Scale

Once we make these models we can then make a set of predictions and test the fit. That is, we may ask the question, "Which of these two models do the facts fit best?" Whichever model the facts fit best would then be assumed to be the better, the more acceptable model.

The Two Sets of Predictions

The Evolution Model	The Creation Model
Galaxies Changing	Galaxies Constant
Building Up Life Evolving from Non-life Continuum of Organisms	Breaking Down Life Only from Life Distinct Kinds of Organisms
New Kinds Appearing	No New Kinds Appearing
Beneficial	Harmful
Creative Process	Conservative Process
Earth Billions of Years Old	Most Data Indicates a Young Earth
Innumerable Transitions	Systematic Gaps
Ape-Human Intermediates	No Ape-Human Intermediates
Quantitatively Superior to Animals	Qualitatively Distinct from Animals
Slow and Gradual	Contemporaneous with Man

Which model do the facts fit best? They both use the same evidence, but they definitely have different interpretations of that evidence. By analyzing them closely we see that the Creation Model fits the known facts best. Every law of science, every known process of nature and all the physical evidence is either explained or predicted by the Creation Model. No law of science, no known process of nature nor any of the physical evidence, except by making up pretty stories, can be explained or predicted by the Evolution Model. Therefore, from a strictly scientific view we would say that the Theory of Special Creation is the better, the more acceptable, view. Conversely, the various theories of evolution are actually refuted by the known evidence—facts, laws and processes.

How do these two interpretations influence society as a whole? **Do these interpretations influence society as a whole?** You bet they do! The next chart shows us strong examples of how these two world-views, based upon the acceptance of creation or evolution, do influence our society!

Evolution	Creation
Abortion and Euthanasia	Meaning and Value of Life
Pornography and Situational Ethics	Absolutes and Standards of Conduct
Homosexuality and Perversion	Marriage and Family
Lawlessness, Anarchy and Socialism	Laws, Rules, Roles and Purpose
Naturalism and New Age	Christian Conservationism

How Does All This Tie to the Gospel?

There are many verses that refer to those people who will question creation and to those whose minds will be corrupted, led astray from the truth.

While I would never deny the truth of spiritual warfare occurring in

13

heavenly places (simply read the Book of Daniel), I would also promote that the majority of spiritual warfare, that is **51%** or more, occurs between our ears. Carefully read some of the verses which are most often used to describe spiritual warfare and you will see what I mean.

In 2 Corinthians 11:3, we find, "But I am afraid, lest as the serpent deceived Eve by his craftiness, your **minds** should be led astray from the simplicity and purity of devotion to Christ."

In 2 Corinthians 10:3-6, we read, "For though we walk in the flesh, we do not war according to the flesh, for the weapons of our warfare are not of the flesh, but divinely powerful for the destruction of fortresses. We are destroying **speculations** and every lofty thing raised up against the **knowledge** of God, and we are taking every **thought** captive to the obedience of Christ, and we are ready to punish all disobedience, whenever your obedience is complete."

When we read "destruction of fortresses (strongholds)," we could easily insert the term "satanic strongholds," the places which imprison the minds of men. The word translated "speculations" is the Greek word *logismous*, which means "reasonings" or "imaginations." We are then told that there are things which are lifted up in opposition to the knowledge, the *gnoseos*, of God. We are further exhorted to take every thought, every *noema*, captive to the obedience of Christ. This word means "devices of the mind." We should conclude then that much of spiritual warfare involves a battle for the mind.

Every thought we think is either going to be in obedience to God or in disobedience to God. These verses allow us to see the importance of the mind and our decisions as they relate to spiritual warfare. We punish disobedience when we refuse to think satanic thoughts, when we refuse to think in disobedience to God, when we think God's thoughts after Him. We do this when, as Paul describes it, our obedience is complete.

Jesus says that a belief in creation is not an option for the mature believer. In John 5:45-47, Jesus was addressing members of the Sanhedrin, the ruling body of the nation. He said to them, "Do not think that I will accuse you before the Father; the one who accuses you is Moses, in whom you have set your hope. For if you believed

Moses, you would believe Me; for he wrote of Me. But if you do not believe his writings, how will you believe My words?"

Jesus used an ancient form of argument which they all understood. Any mention of Moses was a reference to his most famous book, the Book of Genesis. Any reference to Genesis was a reference to the creation story contained in it. What Jesus said that day was that if you do not believe in creation, you have no need for Christ. If you believe that you came from mud to man over millions of supposed years during which death was common, then the death of one man on a cross is meaningless. If, on the other hand, you believe that death entered the universe only because of the sin of mankind, then the death of one sinless man on a cross can atone for the sins of the world.

Finally, how does all this tie to the Gospel? In the Book of Revelation 14:7, we are told what the eternal gospel is, "Fear God, and give Him glory, because the hour of His judgment has come; and worship Him who made the heaven and the earth and sea and springs of waters." We may then summarize the entire eternal gospel in just three words, "Worship the Creator." We have a creature-Creator relationship with God.

What Do We Do with This Information?

Allow me to introduce you to one of the most universally accepted principles in all of science, it is the Principle of Certainty. We all like to be certain don't we? We all want to be certain that we married the right person. We all like to be certain that we are dressing the correct way. But, what is the problem? The problem is that no person may be absolutely certain about anything. Why? Because, in order to be absolutely certain about something, you would have to have complete, total, 100% knowledge about it. There could not be one thing that you did not know about it. If there were even one thing that you did not know, and then you found out about it, it could completely change your decision about something.

Now apply the Principle of Certainty to the acceptance of evolution and creation. The evolutionist accepts evolution by faith. It is a religion. The evolutionist believes that evolution is true, but he cannot be certain that he is right. He believes that it is true, but there is plenty of information that he does not know. Therefore, he believes in evolution by faith and denies the existence of anyone who can know all that there is to know.

What about the creationist? The creationist believes in creation by faith. The creationist has tons and tons of evidence to support his position, but he still does not know all there is to know. Therefore, he believes by faith. What is the difference between the two? The difference is that the creationist knows the One who does know it all. The creationist has a personal relationship with the Creator of the universe. Watch what happens. The Creator does know it all, and therefore, He is certain. The faith of the creationist is based upon the certainty of the One he knows, and therefore, his faith is certain.

What is better: a faith based in uncertainty and always will be; or, a faith based in certainty and always will be? Obviously, the faith based in certainty is a superior faith.

What Is Our Purpose?

There are three statements which will serve well everyone who uses them. First, no one can create anything greater than themselves. Second, no one creates without purpose. Third, only the one who creates an object may define what it's purpose is.

Even if I could make something that could do everything that I can do and knows everything that I know, would it be greater? No. At best it would only be equal to me. I cannot teach something that I do not know. This is the reason why man cannot make himself better.

Have you ever gone into an antique store and picked up a tool that was used 200 years ago and asked yourself the question, "What did they ever do with that?" The truth is, that 200 years ago someone made it less than themselves. They made it with a purpose, which it probably fulfilled quite well. The fact that we do it differently or faster today is irrelevant. Because they were the one that made it, they were the only one that could define what its purpose was.

One of the great questions of life is, "What is my purpose?" The Bible says that God made man and woman in order to have fellowship with Him. You cannot define the word *fellowship* as a one-way street.

Fellowship is, by definition, a two-way street. When you finally come to realize that the Creator of the universe exists, you come to realize that He has been wanting to talk to you, love you and hug you all your life. What will be your response? If you fulfill your purpose, then you talk to Him, love Him and hug Him back. It only gets better and better from then on; because once you talk, love and hug Him, you come to realize how much more He has been wanting to talk, love and hug you, and the cycle just keeps getting better and better.

What happens to people when they refuse to fulfill their purpose? They go flying off into man-made philosophies called evolution.

Does It Make a Difference?

You bet it does! Just read these quotes from atheists:

> As were many persons from Alabama, I was a born-again Christian. When I was fifteen, I entered the Southern Baptist Church with great fervor and interest in the fundamentalist religion; I left at seventeen when I got to the University of Alabama and heard about the evolutionary theory (E. O. Wilson, *The Humanist*, September/October 1982, p. 40).

> I am convinced that the battle for humankind's future must be waged and won in the *public school classroom* by *teachers* who correctly perceive their role as the *proselytizers of a new faith*: a *religion* of humanity that recognizes and respects the spark of what theologians call divinity in every human being. These teachers must embody the same selfless dedication as the most rabid fundamentalist preachers, for they will be *ministers* of another sort, utilizing a classroom instead of a pulpit to *convey humanist values in whatever subject they teach*, regardless of the educational level—preschool day care or large state university. The classroom must and will become an arena of conflict between the old and the new—the rotting corpse of Christianity, together with all its adjacent evils and misery, and the *new faith of humanism*....

It will undoubtedly be a long, arduous, painful struggle replete with much sorrow and many tears, but humanism will emerge triumphant. It must if the family of humankind is to survive (J. Dunphy, "A Religion for a New Age," *The Humanist*, January-February, 1983, p. 23 and 26).

GREAT QUESTIONS IN GENESIS 1-11, PART 1

What Does Genesis Mean?

The word *genesis* means "beginnings." The opening verse of the Bible is normally translated, "In the beginning God created the heavens and the earth." This translation has led some to think that the beginning occurred at some very distant time and that perhaps millions or billions of years have elapsed since the initial creation. When translated, "in the beginning" is *bereshith*, which would be better thought of as meaning, "At the beginning," and that this is *Creatio Ex Nihilo*. This would lend a more accurate meaning to the word and the concept being conveyed, that of a recent creation.

The very first verse of Genesis tells us many things. Scientifically, it declares the universally accepted concept of the space-mass-time continuum. If one had a beginning, then they all began at the same time. If space, mass and time are eternal, then there is no Creator and all the complexity of this universe came about only by random chance.

In addition, the first verse clearly declares four great truths. First, God exists; that is, He is a reality, the only thing that is really real. All other things are temporal. Second, that He is eternal, transcendent and pre-existent from His creation. Third, that He is the only Creator and there is no other. Fourth, that He is sovereign in His powers, there is no one which may overrule Him. Indeed, the word used for God in Genesis 1:1 is *elohim*. This is a plural word used to describe a single God. It is, therefore, a uni-plural word used to describe His unity and His majesty. In the Hebrew mindset this means that our God is too big to even be described by a plural word.

In the Book of Genesis there are fourteen listed origins. These origins are the starting place for specific entities.

1) The **Origin of the Universe**: It accounts for the space-mass-time continuum, consistent with the First Law of Thermodynamics. The universe had to come into existence whole and complete; it could never have been any less than it is.

2) The **Origin of order and complexity**: These do not arise from disorder or chaos, consistent with the Second Law of Thermodynamics. Everything goes downhill by spontaneous degeneration. An input of energy does not increase order. Only an input of intelligence increases order.

3) The **Origin of the solar system**: Again, you cannot get something for nothing.

4) The **Origin of the atmosphere and hydrosphere**: These items have never been proven to occur any place else in the universe.

5) The **Origin of life**: This is consistent with the Third Law of Thermodynamics which says that life only comes from life and after its own kind. Something or someone must start life. It is too complex to start by random chance working on inanimate matter.

6) The **Origin of man**: Man did not evolve, but is a unique creation of the Creator God. Man is the only thing in the universe which is made in the spiritual image of God.

7) The **Origin of marriage**: God's original plan was one man and one woman united for a lifetime in opposition to the perversions of this present world. God did not make Adam and Steve and tell them to go recruit.

8) The **Origin of evil**: Evil is allowed by God as a temporary situation to establish free will and personal responsibility while revealing Himself as Redeemer. If we did not have something to resist, we would be weak and not strong.

9) The **Origin of language**: All 6,000 known languages could be easily derived from the seventy given at Babel. Evolutionary linguists

agree that there is a common root to all languages and that each is a highly complex unity.

10) The **Origin of government**: Human government was constituted in Genesis 9 when God turned over responsibility for civil government to man. All human social law stems from this first command concerning capital punishment.

11) The **Origin of culture**: Genesis describes the origination of music, literature, agriculture, etc. We read of the origin for all the social and natural sciences and arts.

12) The **Origin of nations**: There is only one human race with many ethnic appearances. You are either human or you are not. All of the ethnic appearances can be explained by a clear understanding of the historical record and simple genetics.

13) The **Origin of religion**: Every human being knows that there is something greater than themselves. No one can create something greater than themselves. Therefore, man cannot create his own god.

14) The **Origin of the chosen people**: The Jews are the only people to maintain their identity throughout history. Many "great" human cultures have risen and fallen over the millennia; however, only the Jews have maintained their identity in spite of persecution, war, famine, etc.

What Does Genesis Chapter 1:1 Tell Us?

The Bible says that God created everything in a physical vacuum. Other ancient religions discussed creation out of something else; such as earth, air, fire and water.

The words used to describe creation in Genesis 1 are specific as to what they mean. The word *create* (*Bara*), is always used **only** of God, never of man. This is the power to speak into existence material which had no prior existence. The word *make* (*Asa*), is the ability to organize already existing matter into more complex systems and is used for **both** God and man, as used in Genesis 2:3. The word *form* (*Yasar*), is the ability to mold already existing matter into more structured objects, and is also used for **both** God and man. In Isaiah 43:7, all three words are used to describe God's creative power in one verse. Genesis refutes all of man's ulterior concepts when it comes to the meaning of these words.

Likewise, the Book of Genesis refutes the many man-made philosophies of this present world:

It refutes *atheism*, the belief that there is no God, or denial that God or gods exist, because God is declared to be the Creator of the universe.

It refutes *pantheism*, the doctrine that God is not a personality, but that all laws, forces, manifestations, etc., of the self-existing universe are god, because God is shown to be transcendent above His creation.

It refutes *polytheism*, the belief in more than one god, because it clearly states that there is only one God Who created everything.

It refutes *materialism*, the philosophical doctrine that matter is the only reality and that everything in the world, including thought, will, and feeling can be explained only in terms of matter, because it declares that matter had a specific beginning and Beginner.

It refutes *dualism*, the theory that there are two mutually antagonistic principles in the universe, good and evil, because God is recognized as the only One Who created.

It refutes *humanism*, the modern, monotheistic, rationalist, faith movement that holds that a man is capable of self-fulfillment, ethical conduct, etc., without recourse to supernaturalism, because God, not man, is the only ultimate reality-the only thing that is really real.

It refutes *evolutionism*, the faith in the correctness of the various theories that man evolved from a single cell slowly and gradually over a long period of time to what he is today, because the invisible God and His eternal attributes are clearly seen through the things which He created abruptly, not slowly and gradually over a long period of time.

What Does Genesis Chapter 1:2 Tell Us?

"and (*waw*,) the earth was (*hayetha*)"

This verse refers to the state of the earth as it was first created and as it existed on the first day. With only minor exceptions, none of which truly contradicts this position, the church fathers are in agreement. Both Luther and Calvin strongly agreed on this point.

This verse clearly states that the earth was not something left over from an earlier creation "and (or which) became" something else. Each verse in Genesis 1, except for Genesis 1:1, begins with **and**, *waw*, clearly demonstrating that there is a sequential continuity from one verse to the next. Each creative act, each day, is an immediate follow up to the prior one. God Himself says as much when He defines each day by a specific number and the notation of one rotation of the earth for each day mentioned. The seven days constitute a pattern or type by which we are to live out our lives.

"without form and void [formless and empty, unformed and unfilled] (*thohu wavohu*)"

This phrase is best rendered as "unformed and unfilled." God did not create the earth in vain, nor was it created to be a waste place. He created it to be finished and filled promptly. Genesis Chapter 1 describes the sequence by which God brought completion to the unformed earth and living creatures to fill its empty surface. The initial creation consisted of the basic elements without inhabitants. This matter was then to be fully formed and filled in the hands of the Potter.

"and darkness was upon the face of the deep"

In Isaiah 45:7, we find the verse, "I form the light, and create darkness" which supports this verse further. In this verse we see then that it is the concept of incompleteness, not evil, which is being described.

"the Spirit of God was *moving* [hovering, brooding] (*merachepheth*) over the surface"

It is best to render this word as "brooding"; not as a person agonizes over a problem, but in its agricultural form, as a chicken broods over an egg. This is the start of the earth's rotation. The Holy Spirit is hovering, covering, preparing and energizing the earth in order to finish forming and filling it. As a chicken turns her eggs in order to incubate them, so the Holy Spirit incubated the earth and started its rotation so that later no part of it would be hidden from the heat of the Sun.

What Does Genesis Chapter 1:3-5 Tell Us?

Genesis 1:3-5 clearly shows that it is God's Word which brings light. As shown in verse 1, the Father is the Source of all things; in verse 2, the Holy Spirit is the Enabler of all things; and in verse 3, the Word is the Revealer of all things. It demonstrates that God **only** separated the light from the darkness which was "good" and perfectly suited for His purposes. It is here that God defines His terms: darkness equals night and light equals day.

There is a total misconception in the minds of people who wish to always equate the word *darkness* with the concept of evil. In Isaiah 45:7, God declares that He is "The One forming light and creating darkness, causing well-being and creating calamity; I am the Lord who does all these." This statement does not equate darkness with evil. Rather, it is drawing a comparison that God is the One who creates the physical realities of light and darkness, and the One who brings peace and judgement. Physical darkness is simply the absence of light.

God could never be the author of moral evil. Isaiah is also writing shortly after the time of Zoroaster and his teaching that there is a dualistic religion. Zoroaster taught that there are two gods, one good, the other evil. Isaiah 45:7 leaves no room for any such dualism.

This verse also relates that God starts a formula which determines that each rotation of the earth is a 24-hour day. This pattern is continued throughout Genesis 1. This verse also initiates the pattern for human endeavor of work and rest each day; as well as six days of work and one day of rest each week. In the Old Testament economy, the Jew had to work six days in order to earn one day of rest. At the Cross, the New Testament believer is admonished to rest one day in order to go out and work six. Every parable about the final return of the Master says that only the worker who is found working will be declared to be good and faithful.

That Each Day of the Creation Week Was a Literal 24-hour Day.

Many well-meaning Christians have adopted the Day-Age Theory or Gap Theory as a means of believing in evolution within a biblical context. They declare that the days described in Genesis 1 are not normal 24-hour days, but are long ages of time. They state that each day in Genesis 1 actually represents millions or billions of years of time. These people are either theistic evolutionists or progressive creationists. They have allowed themselves to be bullied by secular scientists into abandoning the *prima facie* meaning of the words used in Genesis 1. They have compromised the Bible with evolution theory. These are people who, in general, think that God used the process of evolution to create all the things that we see around us today. The primary argument for the acceptance of this position is that the word *day* **can** (not **must**) be used either literally or figuratively in the Bible. If, however, *yom* (day) as used in Genesis 1 refers to all or part of literal 24-hour day, then their belief is wrong.

In order to determine which view is correct we must look diligently at the evidence. The two best sources for information on the meaning of Hebrew words are the lexicons of Brown, Driver and Briggs and Koehler and Baumgartner. Although tedious, the question is too important to study quickly. In Brown, Driver and Briggs, there are seven primary meanings for the word *yom* (day). The list follows:

1. Day, opposite of night. Gen. 1:5, 15, 16, 18

2. Day, as a division of time.

    a. working day

    b. a day's journey

    c. to denote various acts or states such as seven days. Gen. 7:4

    d. day as defined by evening and morning. Gen. 1:5, 8, 13, 19, 23 and 31

    e. day of the month

    f. day defined by substantive, infinitive, etc., such as "the snowy day"

g. particular days defined by proper name of place, such as the sabbath day

h. your, his, or their day, as in the sense of the day of disaster or death: "your day has come"

3. The day of Yahweh, as the time of his coming in judgment

4. The days of someone, equaling his life, or his age: "advanced in days"

5. Days

   a. indefinite: some days, a few days

   b. of a long time: "many days"

   c. days of old: former or ancient times

6. Time:

   a. vividly in general sense as in the "time of harvest"

   b. used in apposition to other expressions of time, such as a "month of days" equals a "month of time"

7. Used in phrases with and without the prepositions

   a. such as with the definite article, meaning "today"

   b. in the expression "and the day came that ," meaning, "when"

   c. in an expression such as "lo, days are coming"

   d. in construct before such verbs, both literally, *the day of,* and (often) in general sense—*the time of* (forcible and pregnant representing the act vividly as that of a single day)." Under this definition is listed Genesis 2:4

   e. day by day (*yom yom*)

   f. in expressions such as "all the days" meaning **on** a particular day

   g. in an additional phrase with *bet,* meaning **on** a particular day

   h. with *kap,* meaning as, like the day

i. with *lamed,* meaning on or at the day

j. with *min,* meaning since the day or from the day

k. with *lemin,* meaning since the day

l. with *'ad,* meaning until the day

m. with *'al,* meaning upon the day

Koehler and Baumgartner divide their list into ten different headings:

1. Day, bright daylight, as opposite of night

2. Day, of 24 hours (Gen. 1:5)

3. Special days, such as the "day of prosperity," or the "day of adversity"

4. Yahweh's day

5. Plural of day, such as "seven days"

6. Plural of day, such as "the days of the years of your life"

7. Plural of day in a usage to refer to a month or year

8. Dual, such as in the expression, "a day or two"

9. With the article, "that day"

10. With a preposition such as bet, "on the day," or "when"

It is obvious to even the most casual reader that the natural interpretation of the word *yom* (day) is as a normal day with a 24-hour duration. Nowhere do we see here the support for the idea that the days of creation contained in Genesis 1 are equal to vast amounts of time.

The word *day* is used figuratively in many later verses of the Bible. The point that it is used figuratively in **other** portions of the Bible does not mean that it is used figuratively in Genesis 1. Most notable is that the lexicons show that when *yom* is used in the general sense of *time* it is **always** used in conjunction with a qualifier that demonstrates that time is being counted in literal 24-hour days; such as, "a month of time." We see then that *yom* cannot be defined as an indefinite period of time, which would be required by theistic evolutionists. *Yom* must refer to definite days or periods of days.

There are other points to consider. Each day in Genesis 1 is accompanied by a numerical adjective. **Nowhere** in the Old Testament is the word *yom* used with a numerical adjective to mean anything but a literal 24-hour day. Therefore, obviously from contextual usage, the word *yom* cannot be used with a numerical adjective and mean anything other than a literal 24-hour day.

It is clear that Adam and Eve lived through the seventh day, the day that God rested. It was a perfect day. If it were millions of years long, then certainly Adam and Eve could not have survived it and lived on after it.

Some people point to 2 Peter 3:8, "But do not let this fact escape your notice, beloved, that with the Lord one day is **as** a thousand years, and a thousand years **as** one day." They erroneously suggest that this verse supports the Day-Age position. The obvious context of this verse is that it deals with God's long suffering with sinful man. For God to suffer with us over thousands of years is no different than for one of us to suffer with the peculiarities of another human for a few days. For Him to deal with us over six thousand years is no different than for one of us to deal with another for six days. I may not like you, but I can put up with you for six days, if I know that there will be a specific end to that period.

In addition, the word used in 2 Peter 3:8, *as* or *like* means "similar to," not "equals." The verse uses metaphor to draw an analogy, not to equate the words being used. The verse tells us that to an eternal God a thousand years is "similar to" a day for a human being. 2 Peter 3:8 actually disproves the Day-Age position. It shows us that things which we perceive must take vast amounts of time, using only human reasoning, were in fact accomplished by God in only one day. We see that God may do any amount of work that He wishes to do, in any amount of time He chooses to do it in. He is not limited by time, since He is the Creator of time.

Those who would accept the Day-Age or Gap Theories also have strong theological problems. If what they believe were true then death came before sin. The Bible is quite specific that the first death came after sin; as a consequence, as a result and as a judgment for sin.

If there were a god who could create the earth with life forms on it, but those life forms could become so evil that this god had to destroy them and start over; then that god could be omnipresent, but he could not be omniscient nor omnipotent. If there were a god who had to grope his way through bringing the universe and life into existence over a long period of time, then he is a weak god. If there were a god who could not save even a remnant, then he would certainly not be the God described in the Bible. The God revealed to us in the Bible is omnipresent, omniscient and omnipotent. He is One who is always able to do anything that He chooses to do, and He is always able to save a remnant.

Finally, each day in Genesis 1 is defined by God as being one rotation of the earth, "and there was evening and there was morning, a fourth day." Certainly there could not have been millions of years of night followed by millions of years of daylight. Each day of Genesis 1 is described twice, once by numerical adjective and once by physical rotation, as being a literal 24-hour day.

We might consider what other word God could have used to describe days in the week of creation. He could have used the Hebrew word *dor*, meaning "ages" or "vast periods of time" but He did not. He used the *day* because that is what He meant. "For in six days the Lord made the heavens and the earth, the sea and all that is in them, and rested on the seventh day; therefore the Lord blessed the sabbath day and made it holy" (Exodus 20:11).

GREAT QUESTIONS IN GENESIS 1-11, PART 2

Did Adam and Eve Fill or Refill the Earth?

The Hebrew word *umilu* means "to fill," "to fulfill" or "be filled." It never means "to refill" or "to replenish." Of the more than 300 references in the King James Version of the Holy Bible, the word *umilu* is translated as "replenish" only seven times, all of which could be substituted for with the word *fill*.

What was the purpose of filling the earth to be? As Malachi 2:15 shows, it was to promote the nurturing of godly children, who would raise up godly children. Godly families which would have fellowship with Him was God's purpose for humankind. First Thessalonians 2:12 and Hebrews 2:10 show that the act of filling the earth would bring many people into His Kingdom.

Some people are concerned about over population of the earth; but they fail to understand that God promises that Jesus will return prior to man completely destroying this planet or himself. God gave Man the creation covenant to rule and steward wisely His earth.

What Does the Cultural Mandate "To Subdue" and "To Have Dominion (Rule)" Mean?

"To subdue" and "to have dominion" are military terms which simply say first conquer, then rule. First, we are to intensively and extensively study the earth; all of it's processes and systems. This is science—diligent study to increase the body of knowledge and understanding of phenomena. Second, we are to use this understanding to benefit all of the earth's inhabitants. This is also technology—the application of knowledge for development of the earth's resources to benefit mankind. This Cultural Mandate incorporates all of the productive pursuits for mankind. We see this in our daily lives and call it research and development or analysis and application. These commands establish mankind as the stewards over the earth and all it contains, as we shall see later in this book.

Were All Men, Women and Animals Vegetarians before the Flood of Noah? Should People Be Vegetarians Now?

Genesis 1:29-30, stipulates that all animals and people were given only green plants to eat. These two verses clearly indicate that green plants were to be as nutritious as meat to both mankind and animals. Genesis 9:3, goes on further, however, to state that **now**, that is after the Flood of Noah, people were to eat animal flesh as well, which was then given to them in the same way as the green plants had been, provided only that the blood was excluded.

Following this command, God places the instinctive fear of man into the animals to protect them from being eaten into extinction. Animal flesh was given to man to eat because over time the earth began to lose it's fertility and plants were becoming less and less nutritious. Think about it: which would you rather eat, an acre of grass or a one pound steak? The purpose in having man eat meat is so that the animals will spend their time concentrating food for human consumption. Animals save us time which we use for other things besides food gathering.

What was the "Original Sin" of Mankind in Genesis 3?

Original sin did not occur when Adam and Eve ate of the fruit of the tree of the knowledge of good and evil. That was just an outward physical manifestation of a sin which had already occurred inside. Original sin was not when Adam and Eve decided to be rebellious or disobedient or to be like God. [Original sin occurred when Adam and Eve challenged God's veracity.]

When Adam and Eve decided that they had a **right to decide** whether or not God was telling the truth, they sinned. All thinking is going to be done in obedience to God or in disobedience to God. They decided that they would not think in obedience to God. They decided that God was a liar and they sinned. When they chose to make that decision, they **initiated human autonomy**. The word *autonomy* means "law unto self." They rejected God's Law and wrote their own law.

We all either accept God's Laws as our laws or we will make our own laws. If you think that this kind of thinking is something new, it isn't. Rejecting the Creator and His authority initiates evolutionary thinking, the thinking that God does not exist. If you think that evolutionary theories came into existence only in recent times, you are quite wrong. When the Apostle Paul went to Athens as recorded in Acts 17, he treated the Greeks as evolutionists because the Greeks were evolutionists. The ancient Greeks and Romans believed that people evolved; they believed that even the gods evolved. In the century before Christ, a Roman named Titus Lucretius Carus wrote a six volume set of books in which he outlined the basic tenets of Darwinism.

We can trace evolutionary theories back even further. Note what it says in Judges 17:6 and Judges 21:25. When they had no one to rule over them each man did what was right in his own sight or eyes. What does that mean? It means that "I" write the rules.

What is the one thing which you must have in order to have law? You must have a lawgiver. If there is no God, then all things are permissible. Consider the statements which summarize the prevailing philosophy of the past four and a half decades. In the '50s and '60s it was, "If it feels good do it." In the '70s it was, "If it doesn't hurt someone else, it's okay." Finally, in the '80s and '90s it became, "Even if it does hurt someone else, it's still okay." Why? Because "I" make the rules.

The creationist's belief is that there is a God Who is the absolute authority in all things. That "He" wrote the laws, rules, roles and purposes. One of the great questions in life is, "Do you accept the rules, roles and purposes He has for you?" Evolutionary thinking then comes from not thinking God's thoughts after Him.

Who Are "The Sons of God," "Giants" and "Mighty Men of Old, Men of Renown" Found in Genesis 6:1, 2 and 4?

"The sons of God" (*bene elohim*) can neither be saved persons, as in John 1:12, nor any men in a physical sense, for Adam was the only physical man made by God. The only obvious and plausible description would be that of Adam (Luke 3:38) and angels (Psalms 148:2,5 and 104:4). The words *bene elohim* are used three other times in Scripture: Job 1:6, 2:1 and 38:7, and these verses clearly refer to angels.

The words *bar elohim* are used in Daniel 3:25 and clearly refer to an angel or a theophany. Likewise the words "sons of the mighty" (*bene elim*) are used in Psalms 29:1 and 89:6, and again clearly refer to angels.

There can be no doubt then that these "sons of God" are fallen angels since they are acting in opposition to God's plan. This position agrees with the LXX, Josephus, ancient Jewish commentators and early Christian commentators. Angels always appear in the masculine form as in Genesis 18:8 and Hebrews 13:2, but Jesus said in Matthew 22:30 that they neither marry nor are given in marriage. It is also apparent from Scripture that angels do not have genetic information which could be passed on to others.

Satan and the fallen angels would, as part of their schemes, want to corrupt the human population, so as to prevent the birth of the Promised One, as prophesied by Lamech in Genesis 5:29.

The word *take* or *took* (*laqach*) is a common verb which can have any noun as its object, and *wife* or *woman* (*ishah*) refers to any mature woman regardless of her marital status. The problem which arises is, could a mixed angel-man offspring be saved? Would God even allow such a union to occur, even if it were possible? No! When God reflects upon the situation at that time He says that Man has both flesh and spiritual essence, but that his flesh has become no better than an animal (Genesis 6:13 and 7:21).

What then produced the violence, wickedness and abnormalities of the people described in Genesis 6? What is the resolution to solve this situation? It is quite simple, the children were all fully human offspring of truly human parents. Their parents were entirely human, but humans who were freely willing to be recruited, directed and controlled by fallen angels who were manipulating them for Satan's benefit. Satan cannot create, but he can manipulate that which already exists and he can counterfeit the things of God's creation.

Satan can see the genetic makeup of people and he knows which ones have the genetic material necessary to produce large stature. Then just like a dog breeder, he can cause willing humans to "breed" in order to produce people of greater and greater size. His plan was to corrupt totally the human line in order to prevent the birth of the sin-less Son of God.

One element concerning the nature of the sinful actions of these fall-en angels was that they compounded their sin. These angels left "their own habitation" or "first estate;" they not only tried to cause people to sin, but they actually attempted ancient genetic engineering of the human race (Jude 6, 7). For this double crime they are now confined in Tartarus awaiting final judgment (1 Peter 3:19, 20 and 2 Peter 2:4).

"Giants" (nephilim)

Gigantism is common among plants and animals in the fossil record. The root word for *giants (nephilim)* is *naphal* which means "fall" and refers to the fallen state of their demonic heritage. The LXX translated the word into Greek using *gigantes*. The same word is used of the giants seen in Canaan (Numbers 13:33).

These giants' physical stature is easily explained by simple known principles of the Laws of Genetics using mutations and recombinations of human genetic information. The wide variation for size in humans has existed from the time of creation within the human gene pool. Gigantism may occur by fortuitous random combinations or by controlled genetic manipulation, that is, guided breeding. If human intellect may manipulate genetic material today; then demonic forces could just as easily have done the same thing in the past. This would have been achieved through their recruitment of willing humans to determine which persons when mated with another would achieve the desired result-giants. This is simply ancient genetic engineering.

"Mighty Men of Old, Men of Renown"

These giants were men who were revered for their great strength and great violence, not necessarily for their great knowledge or intellect. The words *mighty* and *renowned* do not necessarily mean good but can mean bad. Here these words are used with acute satire. These men were "mighty" and "renowned" for their evil and their wickedness (Genesis 6:5).

Wickedness and evil are at their greatest when the most notorious of sinners are "men of renown." Men in the Mafia are also mighty men, men of renown. There is a corollary which would be, "Wickedness is great when great men are wicked."

When and Why Was Civil Government Initiated?

All current civil government was initiated by God in Genesis 9:5 and 6. Prior to the Flood of Noah only patriarchal government existed under the supervision of God. Prior to the Flood, God dealt with man directly when it came to judging the breaking of His laws. After the Flood, God transferred the administration of human government to mankind.

In the early chapters of Genesis, the word *nephesh* is used for "breath" (breath of life), "soul" and "life." Life is declared to be in the blood. (Leviticus 17:11) The word *require* as used by God is a judicial command.

Man has an eternal spirit and is the only thing in the universe made in the spiritual image of God. God established human government through the institution of capital punishment. Capital punishment is the basis for all human laws and is based upon this idea: to kill a human is to kill the only thing made in His spiritual image and is, therefore, a personal affront to God. Even the law against running a stop sign is based upon the prevention of murder.

Murder is not a sin against a person, it is sin against God. Once a person is murdered no one can make restitution to that person; they are no longer around to make restitution to. Therefore, the consequence is that the murderer must pay with his own life as restitution to God Himself.

THE ARK OF NOAH

What Was the Physical Structure of Noah's Ark Like?

Using the most conservative figure for a cubit, that of 17.5 inches, the Ark was 438 feet long (300 cubits), 73 feet wide (50 cubits) and 44 feet high (30 cubits). It had a volume of about 1,400,000 cubic feet which is equal to about 522 railroad stock cars. A larger floating vessel was not built until the construction of a steamship called the Great Eastern, which laid the first trans-Atlantic cable in 1865. The Ark displaced about 14,000 tons, with a draft of about 22½ feet (equal to 15 cubits). The Flood is described as covering the highest ground prior

to the Flood by 15 cubits, the exact amount of the Ark's draft.

The Ark could easily have held as many as 125,000 sheep-sized land dwelling air breathing animals, a sheep being slightly larger than the average size animal. There are slightly less than 20,000 kinds or groups of such animals which would have been needed to repopulate the dried out Earth after the Flood. There were three decks inside the Ark, each with about 17 feet of clear height and there were rooms (*qen*), literally meaning "nests" or "resting places," for the animals. Thus, there was plenty of room for all the necessary animals, food and eight people. There was enough room that the family could have had an entire football field next to their living area.

The Ark was made of "gopher wood" which was, apparently, a dense hardwood; perhaps a species of white oak. The Ark was made waterproof by the application of "pitch" to both the outside and the inside. It was to be a place of complete security. It had a window (*isohar*), literally meaning an "opening for daylight," running the full length of the roof. This window allowed for both light and ventilation for all those contained in it.

The Ark (*tevath*) was fundamentally a large rectangular wooden box. *Tevath* is the same word used in Exodus 2:3 describing the "ark of bulrushes;" it is "a vessel for floating." The Ark of Noah is not *aron*, which is the word for The Ark of the Covenant.

Modern marine architects have found that the Ark was, in fact, the single most stable floating object ever conceived. The Ark was almost impossible to capsize since it could have survived being tilted 89 degrees sideways and still right itself automatically. It's length to width ratio of 6 to 1 is used today for all modern ship building because it is the only ratio which causes a ship to automatically turn into the waves for an easy ride, even without the use of rudders, sails or engines. After all, the Ark had no need for navigation or speed, only survivability.

What Are the Spiritual Applications of the Ark?

The Ark is a type for Christ. Lamech prophetically named his son Noah (Rest), because it was through Noah's finished work that we may all enter into Gods "rest" or "comfort." Indeed, Noah can prophetically be seen as a "savior." For one hundred and twenty years, Noah preached the message of repentance; and that only those who entered into the Ark of safety would be preserved with him, saved. It is only through his construction of the Ark that we may all know our Savior. Likewise, only those who enter into the Christ of God will be preserved in the eternity to come.

When we read about the Ark we find that it had only **one** door, only one entrance, located on one **side**. There are many Scriptures which could be alluded to here, but I will only mention a few. We read in John 10:9, "I am the door; if anyone enters through Me, he shall be saved, and shall go in and out, and find pasture." John 14:6 states that there is only one way to salvation. On the cross Jesus was pierced in His side. In 1 John 5:6-11, we find that through the three witnesses; that of the water and the blood which spilled from His side, along with the Spirit, we were provided with the means for eternal life.

The Ark had only one window for light and ventilation which ran the full length of the roof. We know that Jesus is the Light of the World and that the Holy Spirit is the life-giving breath of God. In order to see light and breath fresh air from inside the Ark you had to look up. We must all look up for our redemption draws near.

Dates recorded in the Bible often show that there is more than coincidence in the providential history of God's working with fallen man. The Ark touched Mt. Ararat on the seventeenth day of the first month on the religious calendar (Genesis 8:4), the day later designated as the Feast of First Fruits (Leviticus 23:10-11). The seventeenth day of Nisan consistently deals throughout the Bible with Gods theme of resurrection. There are four events which occur on this specific date in history, the first being the Ark landing on Ararat. The others are: the Jews being resurrected from their march through the Red Sea (Exodus 12 to 14); the eating of the First Fruits in the Promised Land (Joshua 5); and the resurrection of Jesus Christ (The Gospels, 1 Corinthians 15:20-23).

The best definition for the word used to describe Noah's Ark as used in Genesis is *coffin*. God often uses opposite logic to ours to illustrate perfect biblical truths. We usually think of a coffin as containing death and the world outside of it as being alive. In opposition to that kind of thinking, God preserved the seeds of life within the Ark and condemned the Old World left outside to death (Hebrews 11:7). The people and animals inside the Ark were resurrected from the death of the Old World to newness of life in the New World by passing through the waters of baptism in the Flood.

The Ark was made of wood which speaks of His humanity. The trees had to die in order to make a place of refuge and preservation of life. This is true for all three arks mentioned in the Bible: The Ark of Noah (Genesis 6:14-17); The Ark of bulrushes (Exodus 2:3); and, The Ark of the Covenant (Exodus 25:10-16). Jesus died in His humanity for us to have a place of refuge from sin and our lives are preserved eternally in His finished work.

The dimensions of the Ark also speak eloquently of Christ. The length was 300 cubits; 300 is the number of victory in conflict or complete deliverance (Genesis 5:22; Judges 7:7+; 1 Kings 10:17; and Mark 14:3-6). The width was 50 cubits; 50 is the number of anointing, Pentecost or Jubilee. The height was 30 cubits; 30 is the number of authority, maturity, full stature and the age of priesthood (Genesis 41:46; 2 Samuel 5:4; and Luke 3:23).

The Ark and the Lessons for Mankind

The Ark was covered both inside and out with pitch. The word *pitch* (*kopher*) means "to cover" or "covering" (*kaphar*). It is the regular Hebrew word for "atonement" (Leviticus 17:11). *Kopher* may be defined as "appease, make an atonement, cleanse, forgive, pardon and reconcile." *Kaphar* may be defined as "redemption price, ransom payment and satisfaction of debt." Thus the Ark was sealed both inside and out from the waters of judgment with the atoning redemption price, just as the Blood provides a perfect atoning redemption price for Man's sins.

It was God the Holy Spirit Who sealed the door from the outside, for it could not have been the work of the men inside who could not reach it, nor the work of the men outside who refused to help (Genesis 7:16 and 1 Peter 1:5). We know that salvation is the gift of God and God alone. Our works can not save us or anyone else. Like Noah and his family in the Ark, we are hidden in Christ (Colossians 3:3).

40

God sent into the Ark all the clean animals by sevens (3 ½ pairs). The number seven speaks of divine perfection. The fourth male was sacrificed as a thanksgiving offering to God for His faithfulness in saving a remnant, while the three pairs were to repopulate the earth with their kind. The unclean animals were sent by pairs. The number two speaks of "witness." We are told that truth is established by the mouths of two or three witnesses.

The Ark came to rest on Mount Ararat. The word *Ararat* means, "high or holy ground; sacred land." After riding the troubled waters of the Flood, how appropriate that the Ark should come to rest there.

Finally, the Ark had three levels or decks. God also deals with us on three levels—spirit, soul and body.

JOB—A GREAT BOOK OF SCRIPTURE AND SCIENCE

The Book of Job has been described as both the most fascinating and the most forgotten book of the Bible. Most people only stop to look at its literary style, or analyze its philosophical content. The Book of Job, however, is a book describing the nature and work of Satan; supporting the literal interpretation of the creation account in Genesis 1 to 11; and, never deals with the problem of suffering in the lives of righteous people. The Book of Job has two purposes. First, it illustrates God's sovereignty over all the angels whether fallen or not. Second, it declares the foundational importance of the initial creation.

The Book of Job Is a Literary Masterpiece with a Modern Message, Insight and Application

Job is arguably the oldest book in the Bible and Job is declared to be a prophet of God. Job died 140 years after the events recorded in the Book of Job. Allowing time for him to have ten grown children prior to these events, Job would have lived about 2,000 B.C. (Job 42:16). Job lived prior to Abraham, Moses and the establishment of Israel. We know this because there is no mention of any of them, nor of judges, kings, prophets, the Mosaic laws or commandments. We do know that Divine Laws were given to men including Job and Abraham prior to Moses, but they are not recorded (Genesis 26:5; Job 22:22 and Job 23:12).

While religious sacrifices were practiced by Job, no mention is made of the Mosaic sacrificial system or priesthood (Genesis 8:20; Genesis 22:13; Job 1:5 and Job 42:7-9). The Book does describe events recorded in the Book of Genesis which occurred earlier than Job's life, but none from a later time frame.

Is Job then a book of fiction or a true and accurate biographical account? The author claims that his narrative is true. Four chapters quote God verbatim and other chapters describe events which occur in heaven. This would be blasphemous if the statements were not true. The Prophet Ezekiel lists Job as a real person, along with Noah and Daniel; as does the Apostle James (Ezekiel 14:14 and James 5:11). The Apostle Paul certainly thought that Job was a real person and he quotes Job 5:13 in 1 Corinthians 3:19.

The Book of Job is grouped within the "wisdom literature" of the Old Testament Canon. The Book is a wonderful example of Hebrew dramatic poetry. Although not all the statements in the Book express divine truths, we know that each statement is recorded by divine inspiration (2 Timothy 3:16).

The Book of Job is also a magnificent example of syllogism in which the logic goes like this: God punishes sinners; Job has been singled out for punishment; therefore, Job must have committed a special hidden sin. This syllogism is repeated three times and stretches from Chapter 4 to Chapter 26. Each supposed friend of Job presents his first premise to which Job answers them individually. The same procedure is repeated two more times for a total of three rounds. Yet, no hidden sin is ever found in Job's life. In his defense Job bases his innocence upon four firm statements which apply equally well to any believer alive today:

    a. He has been pardoned (Job 7:21).

    b. He has an Advocate (Job 9:33).

    c. He has experienced salvation (Job 13:16).

    d. He has a Redeemer (Job 19:25).

As one studies the Book of Job it is helpful to follow the general outline which is as follows:

    1. Prologue (Chapters 1-2)

    2. Job cries out about his misery and despair (Chapter 3).

    3. The first round of the syllogism (Chapters 4-14)

4. The second round of the syllogism (Chapters 15-21)

5. The third round of the syllogism (Chapters 22-31)

6. Elihu's monologue which attempts to correct everyone else (Chapters 32-37)

7. God's response and science test challenge (Chapters 38-41)

8. Epilogue (Chapter 42)

The question which most people ask when reading the Book of Job is, "Why do the righteous suffer?" But, this question is never addressed in the Book of Job, for that is not it's purpose. At the end of the Book, Job is completely restored and becomes even more prosperous than before; whereas many godly people suffer without ever being restored. Then, too, many people suffer and are never redeemed, while many sinful people enjoy health, success and long life. The answer to the question is to be found elsewhere.

The Book of Job Is a Scientific Masterpiece Which Vindicates the Creation Account of Genesis; Models the Scientific Method; and Contains Many Allusions to Natural Systems and Processes Discovered Only Recently

After Genesis, no other book of the Bible contains more references to the Creator and His creation than the Book of Job. Job assumes God to be the only Creator (Job 9:8) and God alone claims credit for His creation (Job 38:4). We may outline various aspects of Job's belief in creation in the following segments:

I. As Job responds to his accusers he restates many references to the acts of the creation week as recorded in Genesis.

   a. Star formation is described (Job 9:9 and 26:13).

   b. The creation of animals and Man are recorded (Job 12:7-9).

   c. God is shown to be the life, soul and spirit Giver (Job 12:10, 27:3 and 33:4-6).

   d. Adam was a real person (Job 31:33).

II. Sin, the Fall of Mankind and the institution of the Curse are fully recognized in Job.

   a. Sin brought death (Job 34:14-15).

   b. The Curse is said to affect all things (Job 5:7, 10:9, 14:1-4, 15:14 and 25:4).

III. The extent and nature of the Flood of Noah are an accepted fact by Job.

   a. The reason for the Flood was Man's wickedness (Job 22:15-17).

   b. The Flood was a worldwide cataclysm (Job 9:5-8, 12:14-15 and 26:11-14).

   c. The end of the Flood is described correctly (Job 14:11-12).

   d. Job says that God will never again flood the Earth (Job 26:10, 38:8-11).

   e. Even the Ice Age, which occurred right after the Flood, appears to be mentioned in Job (Job 37:9-10, 38:22-23 and 38:29-30).

IV. The creation and dispersion of the 70 nations at the Tower of Babel is an accepted fact in Job.

   a. The scattering of the people is recorded (Job 12:23-25).

   b. Many tribal names from The Table of Nations are mentioned

   - Uz (Job 1:1)

   - Sheba (Job 1:15, 6:19)

   - Ophir (Job 28:16)

   - Cush (Ethiopia) (Job 28:19)

The Book of Job describes the Scientific Method and fully illustrates its use. First, we start with an observation. God firmly states three times that Job is "perfect and upright" (Job 1:1,8 and 2:3). Job, however, declares that he is not sinless, that he understands his need for sacrifice to atone for his sin, and that he believes in a Redeemer (Job 1:5, 7:20-21 and 19:25-27).

Then God proposes a hypothesis concerning the character and

nature of Job stating that his faith is absolute. *Ha' Satan* challenges God to a falsification test. Job passes the first test. Then *Ha' Satan* proposes a second test (Job 1:13-22 and 2:4-7) and Job passes the second test, defending his innocence from any hidden sin. Finally, *Ha' Satan* institutes a third test (Job 2:10, 6:24, 13:23 and 4:12-21+) and Job passes this third and final test, including the claim of man's worthlessness, thus proving himself absolutely faithful. (Job 6:24, 10:2,7, 13:23, 16:17-19, 23:10, 25:4-6, 27:2-6, 38-41 and 42:1-8) We then see the scientific methodology outlined in Job: observation, hypothesis, testing and proven conclusions.

The Book of Job alludes to many of the natural systems and processes which scientists continue to study today.

1. The Water Cycle (Job 26:8, 28:24-27, 36:27-28 and 38:25-28)
2. Geology, Geophysics, Astrophysics
   a. Law of Gravity (Job 26:7)
   b. Earth's rotation (Job 38:12-14)
   c. Continental erosion (Job 14:18-19)
   d. Mineralogy (Job 28:9-18)
   e. Oceanography (Job 38:8,10-11,16)
   f. Astronomy (Job 9:8-9, 11:7-8, 22:12, 26:13, and 38:7, 31-33)
   g. Meteorology (Job 38:22,25-30,34-35)
3. Other physical and social science fields
   a. Optics (Job 38:19,24)
   b. Psychology (Job 38:36)
   c. Physics (Job 38:33)
   d. Electronics (Job 38:35)
   e. Biology/Zoology/Anatomy/Paleontology (Job 38:39-39:30)

What Is the Purpose of the Book of Job?

Job's sufferings had nothing to do with any hidden sin in his life nor for wrongs done during his life. God allowed Job's trials in order to teach *Ha' Satan* what God's Grace may do in a person who has surrendered his life to The Redeemer. God never addresses the question of Job's sufferings. However, God's address to those present does stress the importance of the doctrine of special creation, His providential care and His eternal power, wisdom, purpose and love as seen in His creation.

Therefore, the purpose of the Book of Job is two-fold. First, Job's testimony in Heaven before *Ha' Satan*, the demons and the angelic host bear witness to the awesome plan of God. Second, Job's testimony on earth of God's creation and His providential care oppose the teachings of pantheism, polytheism, secular humanism and evolutionism.

Why Did God Give Job a Science Examination of 77 Questions?

At the end of Job's trials God appears and proceeds not to criticize those present, but rather to simply make His point by giving Job a science test consisting of 77 questions. Why would He do this? Because, it emphasized God's "dominion mandate" given in Genesis. The first set of questions deals with the primeval world and its origin which then refutes Uniformitarianism and Evolutionism. The second set of questions deals with the historicity of Noah's Flood. The third set of questions deals with the present natural systems and processes and asks questions which, even now, are not fully understood by scientists. (Job 38:12 to 41:34)

These questions served to bring Job to humbly declare God as omnipotent and omniscient and that all men everywhere are to be God-centered and not Man-centered. Job's reward for his perseverance was to receive twice the prosperity he had been blessed with before.

Jesus Christ Is Revealed in the Book of Job

Messianic statements are made throughout the Book of Job (Job 9:32-33, 13:15-16 and 19:25-27). As we read through Job we can also see how Christ's rejection by men is paralleled in Job's life (Job 16:10-11, 19:13-14 and 30:10, 16-17). The Messianic passages contained in Psalms 22:7-8,14,16 and Isaiah 50:6 describe both Jesus and Job equally well. Finally, both Job and Jesus became mediators between God and men (Job 42:8).

CREATION IN THE PSALMS

The Book of Psalms Is the Most Glorious Book in the Bible. It Contains the Elements of Praise, Song, Comfort, Anger, Imprecation, Testimony, Prayer, Joy, Hope, Despair, Prophecy, Revelation, Spiritual Blessing and Modern Scientific Insights!

Psalms was the hymnbook of the Jews called "The Hallel Book," "The Book of Praises." The word *psalms* (*mizmer*) means "songs" with musical accompaniment. The Book is actually five books with an epilogue collected into one book.

a.	Book I	Ps. 1 to 41	=	41 psalms
b.	Book II	Ps. 42 to 72	=	31 psalms
c.	Book III	Ps. 73 to 89	=	17 psalms
d.	Book IV	Ps. 90 to 106	=	17 psalms
e.	Book V	Ps. 107 to 145	=	39 psalms
f.	Epilogue	Ps. 146 to 150	=	5 psalms

With the exception of three (Psalms 100, 133, and 150), the Psalms, in some way, deal with conflict. For example, they deal with truth versus lies, righteousness versus sin, believers versus heathens, obedience versus disobedience and God versus *Ha' Satan*.

Psalm One is **the** foundational Psalm which describes the conflict between the righteous man and the wicked man; a battle which goes on even today in the minds of men. Psalm One tells us that the counsel of the ungodly is a man-centered humanistic evolutionary philosophy which denies God, and that man is lost and in need of a Savior.

Psalm One verses 1 through 3 describes that there is only one way and one destiny for the righteous, that which leads to Heaven. Verses 4 through 6 describe the broad way which leads to destruction and the one destiny for the wicked, which leads to Hell (Matthew 7:13-14).

Psalm One begins with "blessed" (*ashere*) meaning "happy" and Psalm 150, the last Psalm, ends on a crescendo of praise (See also Psalms 144:15). Psalm 1:1 stipulates that a happy man does not walk, stand or sit with those who accept a humanistic worldview (see Joshua 1:8). The Psalm outlines the progression men make in accepting the wisdom of this world. The converse of this statement is found in Proverbs 14:12.

The progression outlined in accepting the wisdom of this world goes like this: first, there is the listening to ungodly counsel; second, there is association with the way of sinners; and lastly, there is the total commitment to the seat of the scornful.

To reiterate this outline, it could be rewritten like this. First, a person is drawn away from God's truth by ungodly and pseudo-intellectual philosophy. Once, having rejected truth, a person then writes their own rules, rather than live by God's rules and roles. Finally, having professed to be wise, they become fools and exchange the truth of God for a lie, and give hearty approval to others who do likewise (Romans 1:22, 25 and 32).

Our conclusion, then, is that the godly man is like a tree which brings forth the fruit of the Spirit and he prospers in all that he does (Psalms 2:12). In opposition to this point of view the ungodly man is like wind blown chaff whose secular humanistic philosophy shall cease to exist.

The Book of Psalms Contains Eight Major Creation Psalms with Significant Modern Scientific Importance

Psalm Eight

The first is Psalm 8 which deals with man and the role God has given him in the universe. Verses 1 through 4 praise God for the awesome size and purpose of the universe. They illustrate the truth that we cannot create anything greater than ourselves and that God is greater than and transcendent from His creation. These verses explain that man has corrupted the original purpose of the placement of the stars in the heavens to be signs of God's plan for man. Furthermore, they are a testimony to the existence of the Creator through astrology; and that man has corrupted the purpose of the universe, which displays God's infinite character and attributes, to demean man as insignificant and worthless.

The prophecy of the incarnation of Jesus Christ is seen in verse 4, as well as the plan of God from the foundation of the world. It shows that the earth is the only place of human habitation in the universe, contrary to the opinion of some, and that the earth is the only place from which Christ will reign (Psalms 115:16, Revelation 21:1-3, 22-27). The universe is so big and we are so small, yet God is mindful of each one of us. The human mind is the most complex physical system in the universe; the earth is the most complex planet known; both are central to God's plan.

Verse 5 answers the question, "What is man?" It teaches that man is not an animal; he is made only a little lower than the angels, not a little higher than the apes. There is no evidence to support human evolution, only the pretty stories of those who wish it to be true. Man has a spirit contained in an earthly body which suffers death but may also be saved; neither of which angels can (Hebrews 2:9, II Peter 2:4 and Jude 6).

The verse is prophetic and speaks of Jesus as the Son of Man. The phrase, "a little lower than the angels," could also be translated "for a little time (perhaps 33 years) lower than the angels." Because Jesus conquered death, He is to be crowned with glory and honor.

Verses 6 through 8 tell of the original Dominion Mandate that was given to man but which he has never faithfully practiced (Genesis 1:26-28). Based upon this verse, Matthew Maury set out and found the great ocean currents of the world and became "the pathfinder of the seas." Since the time of the Flood there has been conflict between man and animal (Genesis 9:2-5). However, there is coming a future restoration when the lion will once again lay down with the lamb (Isaiah 11:6-9 and Hosea 2:18).

Verse 9 ends with a repetition of the exaltation found in verse 1. There is an implied section between verses 8 and 9, which is found in Hebrews 2:8-9. After His death, burial and resurrection, Christ will reign and all will proclaim: "Jehovah, our Adonai, how excellent is thy name in all the earth!"

Psalm 19

Psalm 19 deals with the two themes of God's physical revelation in His World (verses 1-6) and His Word (verses 7-14). Verses 1 and 2 deal with the natural revelation which is found in the physical universe. The use of Hebrew parallelism here is to emphasize and demonstrate this truth. Verse 1 tells us that Space and all it contains gives us inexhaustible evidence of God's power and craftsmanship. Verse 2 tells us that Time allows us to know this communication of knowledge, this information about God. The two verses together give us the scientific concept which is called The Space-Mass-Time-(Information) Continuum.

Verses 3 and 4 set the divine standard for both man's heart-attitude toward God and his response to God. The universe teaches us by things which are clearly to be seen and heard (Romans 1:16-32). Thus the scientific principle of cause and effect leads us demonstrably to the Uncaused Cause. Ours is an evidence-based faith. A man's response to this witness measures his relationship to God.

Cause	Effect
Infinite and Eternal	Endless Space and Time
Omnipotent and Omniscient	Endless Power and Order
Omniscience	Endless Knowledge

Verses 5 and 6 mention several specific scientific facts about our sun. We are told that in space and time God has set a tent for the sun. The sun's radiation goes forth and energizes the earth, the solar system and travels on out into endless space. The sun ultimately provides all the power to operate the earth—it powers the chemical, electrical, hydraulic and many other systems on the earth. The existence of the sun demonstrates for us the First and Second Laws of

Thermodynamics. The sun may also be seen as a correlative for Christ; it conquers darkness as the "light" of the world.

In verses 7 through 14 we see that the perfect witness of the creation means that men are without any excuse to deny the existence of God; and, that if the message is rejected, they are without salvation. The creation was made perfect, but the commission of sin made it imperfect. We are told that natural revelation can not save but the written Word does save. The Word is declared to be perfect and true, "words which will not pass away." (Hebrews 4:12, 1 Peter 1:23 and Matthew 24:35) The psalm ends with a prayer recognizing the relationship between the thoughts of our innermost being and the words of our lips.

Psalm 29

Psalm 29 contains within it an ex-Genesis account of events which occurred during and after the Flood of Noah. It opens with two verses giving a description of the faithful angelic host (*bene elim*) giving praise around the throne of God. These angels are "in the beauty of holiness (the sanctuary)." At this time the fallen angels are at work corrupting men on earth.

Verses 3 through 11 are the responses to this praise as the angels recount God's judgments during the Flood. Seven times the "voice of the Lord" is heard, which speaks of His perfect judgments. Seven times the Lord spoke to Noah, each time in perfect grace. Consider this in relationship to the sevens of perfect judgment found in Revelation. Verses 3 and 4 mention the very first thunder which occurred with the very first rain at the time of the Flood (Genesis 7:11-12). Verses 5 and 6 tell of the forests around the world being uprooted and the hills being shaken with earthquakes, landslides and rapid erosion. Verse 7 describes the volcanic activity during the Flood when tens of thousands of volcanoes all erupted at the same time. Verse 8 speaks of the total desolation and destruction of the earth's surface and its preparation to once again bring forth life from death. In verse 9 we see that the final Word of the Lord brings the repopulation of the earth by the plants and animals. Verses 10 and 11 are the epilogue in which the angelic host notes that God did not even have to stand up, to make an effort, to accomplish the work of the Flood; He remains the eternal omnipotent King who encourages and protects all who trust in Him.

Psalm 33

Psalm 33 declares to all who read it that the Word of God is righteous (Verse 4), powerful (Verse 6) and absolutely certain (Verse 9). The psalm is divided into four sections containing 4, 5, 6 and 7 verses each. Verses 1 through 4 are full of exhortation to praise the mighty words and works of God. Here we find the first of the six "new songs" mentioned in the Book of Psalms (Psalms 33:3, 40:3, 96:1, 98:1, 144:9 and 149:1).

The reason for such praise is that the Word of God is right and true, and it will stand forever because He is God (Psalms 119:128). One of the strongest affirmations of God's creative acts as recorded in the Book of Genesis is found in verses 5 through 9. God did not just make the universe slowly and gradually; He spoke it into existence rapidly. The Word, Jesus as Creator, brought this creation into being (Colossians 1:16, Hebrews 1:2-3, Ephesians 3:9 and 2 Peter 3:5).

Verse 6 speaks of the work of the Holy Spirit in creation, "the breath of His mouth," which is the *Ruach Ha'Kodesh*. Verse 7 describes the waters of creation, those to be found both above and below the firmament or expanse. Finally, verse 9 states that with God time is not needed to accomplish His creative acts; He spoke and it simply **was**. This statement counters any possible argument for evolution being compatible with the Bible (Psalms 148:5-6).

Verses 10 through 15 allow us to see God's sovereignty after the experience at the Tower of Babel in which the 70 nations came into being. Verses 10 and 11 contrast the human philosophies of a one world government being instituted at Babel which are for naught; and the counsel of the Lord in which His righteous ones will stand forever. In verses 12 through 15 we see the Lord in control as He sees all things, makes all things and understands all things.

Last, in verses 16 through 22 we see the work of salvation described. Salvation is not found in earthly power or might; it is to be found only in the Lord and in the power of His might. "The eyes of the Lord" describe His perpetual care, concern and covering for those who are His own (Verse 18). The final affirmation is that those who wait upon the Lord shall rejoice in their salvation (Psalms 34:15, Proverbs 5:12, 15:3, 22:12 and 2 Corinthians 16:9).

Psalm 90

Psalm 90, a psalm of Moses just prior to his death, describes God's eternal pre-existent nature and His wonderful plan for man divided into three sections. One of the great dividing lines between Christianity and other religious positions is that only the Bible claims a God Who existed prior to all other things; every other religious document starts with the pre-existence of matter. In verses 1 through 4, Moses recalls both The Fall and The Curse. The Curse is really just the scientifically proven Second Law of Thermodynamics as it applies to all natural systems. Verse 4 speaks of the trivial life span of humans compared with the eternal timeless nature of God.

The second section of verses 5 through 11 compares the span of a human life to the debris carried away with the Flood of Noah; to a single night's dream; and to a grass which grows and then withers. (James 4:14) We see man's Adamic sinful nature exposed throughout our lives recorded in verse 9. Because of the effect of this nature of sin today man is given only 70 to 80 years, "the days of our years."

The third section, verses 12 through 17, speak of true wisdom and salvation. They reveal that true wisdom is found only in God. (1 Corinthians 1:30) Moses ends his psalm with a prayer for God's complete salvation. His prayer actually makes seven specific requests of the Lord which could just as equally be our model today.

Psalm 91

Psalm 91 contrasts the brevity of human life found in Psalm 90 with the "long life" (eternal life) ascribed to the trusting believer. The Psalm is divided into four sections. Verse 1 is an invitation to salvation for anyone who will trust Him. Here God is called the Most High God (*El Elyon*) and the Almighty (*El Shaddai*). He is the One Who is over all things; the Protector and the Sustainer under all things; and the One Who Nourishes and is our hiding place (Psalms 119:114 and Colossians 3:2-3).

Verse 2 records the acceptance of a believer as he responds to God's gift of grace. Verses 3 through 13 have the theme of God's promise of divine protection. These verses are clearly based upon the actual life experiences of Moses and the Hebrew children in the wilderness. In verses 3, 5 and 10 we see the repetition of God's promise that those who obey His health laws will prosper physically (Exodus 15:26). Most important, however, is that God's Truth is our shield against the daily attack of the Great Deceiver (Verse 4, John 17:14, 17 and Ephesians 6:14, 16). It is our God's character that He always saves a remnant. In verse 9 we see that those who dwell in Him are absolutely secure. There can be no safer place than to be in the center of God's will (Proverbs 3:6).

Verse 13 promises protection to the believer, even against the dragon (*tannin*) [Satan], or dinosaurs! (See Job 40:15-41:34) The Psalm ends with three verses of God's personal assurance spoken directly to the believer. These verses are in direct response to the confession of faith by the believer found in verse 2. The knowledge of the Truth brings salvation, healing and deliverance (John 8:31-32).

In verse 15 God makes four promises to the believer. I will answer your prayer. I will be with you-personally with you. I will deliver you, actually "arm with divine armor." I will honor him, the believer (amazing isn't it)! In the last verse God says that the believer will have "long life;" really "length of days" but this means "forever," eternal life with God, the only and infinite source of love in the universe.

Psalm 104

Psalm 104 spans the history of creation from the creation week to the Flood of Noah and on to the post-flood world. The first three verses record the first things which happened in the beginning; the entrance of God into human history as He creates the universe, the Lord is covered (arrayed) in glory and honor and He is clothed in physical light. (John 1:5 and 1 Timothy 6:16) The creation of the angelic host prior to the physical universe is recorded in verses 4-5. (Job 38:4-7)

Mass and energy are interchangeable according to the well known formula of Einstein, E=mc2. **Nothing** may be lost, and in the beginning God concurrently made space-mass-time via His radiating light. He "stretches out heaven" and makes a dwelling place where His essence is centered, a throne surrounded by light. (Eph. 4:10) Yet, God is omnipresent; the entire universe is His dwelling place and this is "seen" by looking at the heavens.

We are told that the earth will not be removed; God has an eternal purpose for it. Verses 6 through 9 give us additional information from outside of the Book of Genesis about the things which happened at and immediately after the time of Noah's Flood. The Flood covered **all** the mountains of the world and was, therefore, a worldwide catastrophic event of God's judgment. Some people have taught that the Flood was only a local event, or more recently, one author has stated that it was only "a local **storm**." If the waters were "standing above the mountains," would they not at least flow into the neighborly valleys? Clearly the Flood was a global event.

We must remember, too, that the mountains which existed prior to the Flood were not like the tall mountains that we have around the world today. You only have to have 1,000 feet of elevation difference in a local area for a hill to be called a mountain. The mountains that existed before the Flood were only 1,000, 2,000, up to 5,000 feet high. They would have been like the California Coastal Range in appearance. They were short enough that a mile of water would have covered them.

In verse 8 we are told of the tremendous mountain building and valley sinking which occurred during the year of the Flood and during the years immediately following the Flood. God also has made a promise that He will never again flood the earth and here we have further confirmation of that because God has set a boundary for sea level (Job 26:10). The Flood was a one time event with a one time purpose.

The world is described as it appeared after the Flood in verses 10 through 35. We see God's providential care for all the life forms which survived the Flood in that they were designed to live in both the pre-flood and post-flood environments. In verses 10 through 15 we find God's methods for providing food for all of His creatures. In verses 16 through 18 each form of life is provided with a place to live. In verses 19 through 23 all life has a plan and a purpose given by God.

Interestingly, we are told that it is God Who creates darkness. Many people associate darkness with evil and wickedness, but this is not always appropriate. There is a darkness which is simply a physical reality and has no evil connotation.

In verses 24 through 30 we see His providential care summarized. We have the mention of Leviathan, a marine dinosaur, probably a species of *plesiosaurus*. Volcanic activity during and after the Flood is described as well. There are over 20,000 volcanoes of the surface of the world and many of these are ancient, possibly dating from the Flood when the earth was cleaved open. Last, in verses 31 through 35 we have a testimony of praise ending with the first *hallelujah* in the Book of Psalms.

Psalm 139

Psalm 139, a psalm of King David, gives us a four-fold view of our Creator God. It is a magnificent Psalm containing blessing, encouragement and exhortation to all believers of all the ages. The Psalm consists of four sections of six verses, each section dealing with a particular aspect of God's all powerful personage. God is shown to be omniscient in verses 1 through 6. God is described as omnipresent in verses 7 through 12. God is declared to be omnipotent in verses 13 through 18. God is also "omni-judicious" in verses 18 through 24. In essence; God knows everything about me, sees everything around me, does everything for me and judges everything within me. This is a personal prayer of King David to the Lord and it should become our personal prayer as well.

If God could know one man better than he can know himself, then God may know the innermost parts of all men. David uses only superlatives in describing God's omniscience. God knows everything, every thought, every movement; He knows our past, present, and future; even before it is a reality. In our finite mind we are unable to comprehend the infinite. We are unable to occupy or even to think of a place where He is not present. (Jeremiah 23:24)

Verses 13 through 18 contain some of the most accurate and modern descriptions of the marvelously complex and ingeniously designed human body; clearly showing God to be omniscient. Man's body is the result of power and information directed by a plan to achieve a complex system, which could not be the result of random chance over eternal time. "My substance" (frame) was made in "secret" (the exact time of conception is secret) and "wrought" (**embroidered**) in the "earth" (my mother's womb) when my "unformed substance" (**embryo**) was conceived. These are, indeed, very accurate and descriptive words to show that among other things, you are human from conception and that life is eternally, infinitely valuable in God's sight.

Last, verses 19 through 24 illustrate the theme of God's holiness and complete requirement for justice. God's foreknowledge of sin does not excuse sinful actions. God is all loving, but He is also all just; therefore, we are to hate the sin and love the sinner, just as He does with us. The last two verses are a prayer in response to the admissions of King David contained in the first three verses; David asks to fully know the mind of God Himself. Isn't that a challenge to any believer today?

The Book of Psalms Contains Many Other Scientifically Accurate Statements Spread Throughout Its Contents

Psalms 103:11-12 speaks of the infinite expanse of the universe. Psalms 95:5, 96:5 and 100:3 declare God's creation of the seas, heavens and men. Psalm 136:4-9 declares that God and God alone is the Creator. Surely then theistic evolution is ruled out when one understands the whole counsel of God (Psalms 119:99 and Psalms 135:5-7).

THE NINE GREAT "PROOFS" FOR EVOLUTION

Proof #1—Evolutionists Claim That "Things" Change over Time, Thus "Proving" Evolution. Do They?

This proof is discussed in three parts which make up the whole. Evolutionists make three claims to support their position that things do change over time. The claims are: that genetic information changes beneficially by random chance over time; that natural selection and survival of the fittest are driving these mutational changes "upward" to produce greater intelligence and complexity; and, that the adaptation of species to new environments demonstrates evolution at work.

Genetics

Evolutionists say that biological life forms change in an "upward" direction, becoming more and more complex, through spontaneous mutation of genetic information. However, the word mutation means by definition "copying error." A mutation is a structural change in the hereditary material which makes the offspring different from the parents. Mutations are errors in copying the genetic codes.

You may copy something perfectly or imperfectly, but you cannot copy something more perfectly. If we copy something perfectly, then there is no change from one generation to the next. If we copy something imperfectly, then the information is degraded or corrupted and the next generation will suffer from the imperfections of the copying processes.

Gene pools contain lots of information but "new" genes, that are "new pieces of information," are never produced. New information does not come into existence without the input from a greater outside intelligence. Mutations are random and not directed. Mutations affect and are affected by many genes and other intergenic information acting in combination with one another. Neither is new information produced simply from an input of undirected energy.

The addition of excess undirected energy will accomplish nothing beneficial; it will destroy the previously existing system. For example: if a computer designed to operate on 110 volt electricity is plugged into a 220 volt power supply it will destroy the computer. But, all that we did was to add excess undirected energy into the computer's system.

The Laws of Genetics are conservative, not creative; these laws only allow for the copying or rearranging of previously existing information which is then passed on in new combinations to the next generation. Even ardent evolutionists like, Dr. Stephen J. Gould of Harvard University, Dr. Niles Eldredge of the American Museum of Natural History in New York and Dr. Colin Patterson of the British Museum of Natural History, have admitted that there are **no transitional life forms found in the fossil record. None!**

Random mutations produce microevolution, which is only variation within a created kind. Random mutations cannot produce macroevolution, which would be the supposed change from one kind into a different kind.

Genetic research which has attempted to force spontaneous mutations has proven to be futile in producing beneficial mutations. Evolutionists cannot adequately answer the question: "Where did the original information that is being copied come from?"

Since 1910, over 3,000 mutations in Fruit Flies have been documented, yet there is no documentation of a Fruit Fly evolving into something else.

Do Things Change Over Time?

Consider ants, horseshoe crabs, bats or algae. Many ant species appear in amber from the Dominican Republic, which evolutionists claim is 25 to 40 million years old. Yet they look exactly the same as they do today. Fossil horseshoe crabs claimed to be 150 million years old are identical to those found alive. The oldest skeleton of a fossil bat, dated as Eocene by evolutionists and supposedly 50 million years old, looks exactly like the skeleton of modern bats. The "oldest" fossils found on earth are said to be blue-green algae colonies one billion years old; yet these fossil colonies seem to be duplicates of living colonies.

There has been an often touted story told by evolutionists about the supposed evolutionary changes that occurred in the English Peppered Moth. They declared that this story "proved" that evolution could be seen at work in nature.

The story goes something like this. During the Industrial Revolution of the 19th Century, the English Peppered Moth changed from a mixed population of individuals that were mostly white with black specks and fewer black individuals with white specks to a population that was mostly black with only a few white. The idea was that coal burning had darkened the tree trunks and buildings in England and that the white individuals stood out against the dark background and the black individuals were camouflaged; thus, whiter individuals were eliminated by birds eating them first and the black were protected and they propagated an ever larger percentage of the total population.

The story is, however, a total hoax! In the 1950's, a British physician, Bernard Kettlewell, wanted to try to prove that evolution was true and that natural selection was at work in nature as Darwin had believed. In order to get his proof he tried to release English Peppered Moths during the day near trees with bark of various colors. He wrote an article for the *Scientific American* magazine and declared that his experiment was evidence of Darwin's predictions. His article has become the foundation of hundreds of textbook references to evolution at work in nature.

In the 1980's evidence was given that this story is a hoax. First, English Peppered Moths are nocturnal and do not fly around during the day when birds might see them. Dr. Kettlewell had to wake the moths up, and in their confusion of seeing daylight, more landed on him than on the nearby trees. Second, the Moths do not land on the trunks of trees where they might be seen by predators (if they were out in the daytime) because they live in the canopies of trees where they are well hidden. Third, the photographs of these moths sitting on tree trunks and reproduced in countless textbooks were staged. The moths were actually dead and had to be glued onto the trees in order to take the now famous photographs.

What does the English Peppered Moth teach us about natural selection? They demonstrate the fixity of species and the natural and easily understood lateral adaptation allowed within a gene pool, fully consistent with the creationist position. The structure of the moth did not change over time. This moth illustrates lateral adaptation, not progressive evolution. We may summarize the factual information about mutations in these five statements.

First, mutations are harmful, since they are, by definition, copying errors. Only a perfect copy of previously existing information is desirable. Anything else is a copying error, and that means that the information will become worse, not better, over time.

Second, mutations are rare and beneficial ones are unknown. You can't get better than perfection. Any copy must either remain perfect, or if a change does occur, then that change would have to go "downhill." Consider these examples. What happens when a story is retold from one person to another in a string of ten people? Do we end up with the original story? If an original cartoon and caption are copied 100 times prior to your receiving it, are the lines a little wavy? Are there black specks on the paper that were not on the original? Has the picture improved or gotten worse for copying? What would happen if a blind, tone-deaf person were to randomly change the tension of the strings on a perfectly tuned piano? Would the piano stay in tune? Would he ever get it back in perfect tune by random chance? These are useful examples of what happens when mutations occur.

Third, mutations do not create new organs; they only modify existing ones. We have never seen a new organ appear fully developed and ready to use. We have seen existing organs become deformed and unusable through mutation.

Fourth, mutations do not accumulate; that is, they do not build, or have an additive effect, one after another to form a chain of major evolutionary changes. Any change that does occur is diluted in the very next generation so that there is no long term net beneficial effect.

Fifth, mutations lead to the wrong kind of change. What occurs is only the deterioration and corruption of the previous information, not the building up of information and structures.

The Laws of Genetics do not fit with the random chance progressively "upward" increase in either intelligence or complexity which the theories of evolution would require. The Laws of Genetics were written by the Creator to maintain and preserve the information that He had encoded in the original kinds as described in Genesis Chapter One.

Natural Selection and Survival of the Fittest

Evolutionists claim that the driving force for the progressive upward increase in complexity and intelligence of living organisms is due to natural selection and survival of the fittest, "nature red [bloody] in tooth and claw" as Charles Darwin put it. Is this position correct, logical or even plausible?

Natural selection was first a creationist argument! William Edward Blyth (1818-1873) in 1835, 24 years before Charles Darwin, stated that natural selection was only a conservative process that removes defective organisms and keeps species pure and strong. Dr. Thomas Huxley, M.D., and known as "Darwin's Bulldog" in England, chastised Darwin for not giving Blyth the credit for the concept. Even though Darwin verbally agreed with Huxley that he should have given Blyth the credit, Darwin refused to do so in print.

Creation believing scientists of the past four hundred years have consistently said that natural selection and survival of the fittest were the methods designed by God to preserve the purity of the created kinds, thus preserving the kinds as closely as possible to the design with which God started. By weeding out the genetically defective, the older and the infirm individuals in a population, those remaining were healthy and strong versus weak and extinct. Wildlife management research done around the world has proven that natural selection and survival of the fittest do not work in nature to produce progressive "upward" evolution, but rather that these mechanisms in nature work to preserve and maintain the purity of the kind.

Predators, which are said to be the ones who "weed" out a population, do not take the defective or infirm only; predators are opportunistic hunters and take any individual, including the best and strongest, regardless of their condition. Predators do not go out and make value judgments. Predators (lions) do not look at the individuals in a herd (antelope) and say to themselves, "That one is genetically defective." Or, "That one is old, so I'll take that one." Predators take prey based upon the opportunity to catch it. If the strongest and most intelligent member of a herd makes a mental mistake and gets isolated from the herd, the predators will take that one first. When a Killer Whale swims through a school of fish it is not the survival of the fittest; it is the survival of the most fortunate —the survival of the luckiest.

Evolutionists propose that the following formula describes their myth: Mutations Cause Change + Nature Causes Change = Observed Evolution. What is the real formula? Adaptation + Imagination = The Myth of Evolution.

Interestingly enough, recent research in the Galapagos Islands, which made Charles Darwin so famous, has shown that small populations often lead to extinction rather than speciation and this has caused evolutionists to demand ever increasing land areas to be set aside in order to prevent extinction from a lack of biodiversity. This would seem to go counter to the prior evolutionary belief that it was isolation in new environments which was the cause of new species.

Evolutionists claim that over time things get bigger, better, faster and smarter. The physical record shows, however, that plants and animals in the past were bigger than they are today. Consider the cockroach, dragonfly and Chambered Nautilus. Today, cockroaches grow up to 2 3/4 inches long, but in the fossil record they are often up to 18 inches long. Today, we have dragonflies that are up to six inches across in wingspan, but in the fossil record we find them with wingspans of up to 50 inches across. Today, chambered nautiluses grow to be 10 ½ inches in diameter, but in the fossil record we find them up to eight feet in diameter. So, things aren't getting bigger, better, faster and smarter. They are getting smaller, worse, slower and dumber.

A 50 inch wingspan dragonfly was found in Italy.

Adaptation of Species

Evolutionists claim that adaptation of species to new environments proves that evolution occurs. It is true that intelligent outside manipulation of breeding can produce new combinations which yield a new specific variety, or sometimes called a "race," of a "kind" of species. The variety produced can only be maintained, however, if the outside intelligence (human beings) continues to guide the breeding process in order to maintain the purity of that variety.

As everyone knows, dogs and cats are indiscriminate breeders and, if left to their own devices, will produce a "Heinz 57" kind every time. You can take the two biggest horses you can find and they will not continue to give birth to ever larger horses. There is a limit

69

which cannot be exceeded. This also works in the opposite direction. If it is possible to breed ever smaller dogs down to "miniature," and then "toy;" shouldn't it be possible to continue the process until dogs became so small that eventually a breed of invisible dogs were produced? This, of course, is nonsense. There is a limit to how small a species may get and still remain viable.

What Charles Darwin observed in the 1800's was the artificial selection that produced many of the purebred varieties that we see today. Artificial selection occurs when people decide which animal or plant will breed with another. Darwin knew that if he stated that artificial selection was occurring in nature by random chance no one would believe him. Therefore, he wrote deceptively that "natural selection" was the driving force of evolution.

Please refer to the comment on the Galapagos Islands above concerning the effect of environment on species. Lateral adaptation within a gene pool is consistent with the creationist position; gene pools may be "pushed" to the edge of the envelope by human breeders but one kind never becomes a different kind.

Pure breeding and hybridization have produced extremes at the edge of the gene pool; but the sugar content of sugar beets and the speed of racehorses have been maximized by breeding in the past and very little additional change is genetically possible in the future.

The ability of life forms to adapt to new environments actually demonstrates that they were designed/created. Only the farsightedness of a perfect Creator could take into consideration all the future factors and design plants and animals to be able to survive under so many varied conditions.

Proof #2—Evolutionists Claim That the Fossil Record "Proves" Evolution. Does it?

The evolutionist uses a false form of circular reasoning to "prove" that he is correct. First, he starts with the assumption that he is correct, by faith. Second, he goes to the other side of the circle, digs up fossils from different places around the world and arranges them in the order he "wants" them to be in. Last, he goes back around the circle and says, "You see, the fossils prove that I am right." This logic is patently illogical.

When the Greeks developed the science of logic 2,500 years ago, they called this kind of reasoning a tautology; that it was circular reasoning that falls under its own weight, that it was patently illogical. If you allow me to rearrange the evidence I can prove anything I want to, can't I? You cannot rearrange the evidence and then claim proof for anything!

If you remember little else from this material, remember this! One of the single greatest differences between a creation-believing scientist and an evolution-believing scientist is that the creationist does not rearrange his evidence and the evolutionist does!

The creationist has no incentive to want to rearrange the evidence. No matter what the evidence is, no matter where the evidence is found, as long as it is found honestly, the creationist has no incentive to move it. We may not understand it now; we may not have the correct interpretation of it now; we may never understand it until He comes back to tell us what it is all about; but we believe that whatever is found honestly will be consistent with a Creator God and we have no incentive to rearrange the evidence. The evolutionist must rearrange his evidence before he claims proof; and that is a monstrous difference!

The evolutionist claims that the fossil evidence is the slow and gradual accumulation over millions and billions of supposed years of dead plants and animals. These remains are supposedly contained in layers which are "in the right [evolutionary] order." This order is supposed to be the order found in the typical Geologic Time Column or Geologic Time Scale so often printed in evolutionary science textbooks. This series of fossil bearing rock layers starts with the present at the top and goes down, or "back in time," billions of supposed years. These charts typically show that single-celled creatures came from nonliving matter (rocks) by random chance; that once alive, these single-celled creatures inherently became multiple-celled creatures; that multiple-celled creatures eventually evolved into man.

What is the truth about the rock layers? The truth is that there is not one location on earth where you can take a pick and a shovel and, starting at the surface, dig straight down and find the rock layers in the "perfect [evolutionary]" order which the evolutionist's claim them to be in. The Geologic Column does not exist in nature; **it only exists in the textbooks and in the minds of those who chose to believe it.** The Geologic Time Column is nothing more than evolutionary speculation and arbitrary opinion. No where in the world is it to be found!

To be fair, there are 26 locations of the surface of the earth where the major layers may be found in the "textbook" order, however, that is only if you look at them from a couple of miles away. If you look at them up close and personal there are many discrepancies to be found in those layers.

More importantly, if there are only 26 locations on the surface of the earth where the layers may be found in the order shown in the textbooks, what do you do about the other million locations on earth where the layers cannot be found in the textbook order?

What do we find in the real world? We find that the rock layers are out of order, upside down, interlaced and missing. Most often we find only two to four layers in any one location. Often these layers are not in the "right" order according to evolutionists. Often we find "older" layers on top of "younger" layers. One such example is Heart Mountain in Wyoming, where the top two layers of the mountain are upside down, according to evolutionary philosophy, and there is 300 million years supposed years missing in between.

How can this be? The evolutionist replies that this is an example of "overthrust." Overthrust is supposed to be a place where a large section of rock layers have been broken off by seismic activity and then pushed up and over the adjacent rock layers. True overthrust is rare and easily detected because when it does occur it leaves a layer of broken rock pieces between the layers of rock which are moving against each other. Note, however, that the amount of pressure necessary to push large volumes of rock up and over other layers would be enough pressure to pulverize the rock being pushed. Also, most "out of order" rock layers do not even have dust in between then. Overthrust cannot explain the many rock layers which are found "out of order" all over the world.

You only find fossils in sedimentary rock. The word sedimentary comes from the word sediment, which is what remains at the bottom of a glass of water after you throw dirt into it. Sedimentary rock was mud which dried out into hard rock. Sediment comes basically from water-carried material, although a small amount may be formed from windblown debris.

I would like for you to consider the following statement and then I will ask you a question. Seventy-five to eighty percent of the entire earth's surface is covered with dried-out mud layers containing trillions of dead plants and animals that all drowned. Does that sound like the result of slow and gradual accumulation over millions and billions of supposed years? Or, does that sound like what we would expect to find as the result of a recent rapid one year long worldwide flood? The fossil evidence is best understood as trillions of dead plants and animals which drowned in a recent flood. Only a worldwide flood such as the Flood of Noah could produce the rock layers which we find covering the earth today.

Many of the fossil layers are found in highly folded or convoluted shapes. Have you ever tried to bend hard flat rock layers? Hard rock does not bend, it breaks. These folded layers of material demonstrate that they were formed by water deposition, and then folded by tectonic activity while they were still wet; and only after they were folded did they dry out into hard rock (Please see Psalm 104:8).

Eighty to eighty-five percent of the rock layers found on the surface of the earth do not have even three of the layers in the "correct [evolutionary] order."

Research conducted in sedimentation laboratories at Colorado State University and in France proves conclusively that in nature sedimentary layers do not form slowly one on top of the other as evolutionists claim; but, rather that sedimentary layers form by growing sideways as the result of sorting by size and velocity as they are extended by water deposition flowing in a specific direction. This is well documented revolutionary research refuting evolutionary thinking.

Have you ever been to a limestone cave full of stalactites and stalagmites? If you go to Carlsbad Caverns in New Mexico, Mammoth Cave in Kentucky or Luray Caverns in Virginia, you will be told that it takes perhaps 10 to 20 million years for a limestone cave to form. Does it?

In the basement of the Lincoln Memorial in Washington, D.C., stalactites up to five feet long were formed in only 45 years. So, I guess it doesn't take 20 million years to get a limestone cave. At Carlsbad

Caverns, the body of a dead bat was found encased in a rapidly growing stalagmite. The body of the bat had not had enough time to decompose before it was covered up. Recent research has demonstrated that in natural caves stalactites and stalagmites grow an average of four inches per year.

Is fossilization a slow process or a fast process? Does it take millions of years to get a fossil? After something is alive and then dies there are only three requirements for fossilization to take place. The dead plant or animal must be buried rapidly. This is obvious in order to prevent decay on the surface. While wind does bury things, it also unburies things just as fast. Only water buries things quickly and buries them well. Next, there must be no oxygen present or decay will still occur. Last, the cavity must remain undisturbed, otherwise oxygen would get in and whatever had not already fossilized would decay.

Fossil fish have been discovered in northern South America and even their gills were preserved. The gills of a dead fish are the first thing to decompose and are usually completely gone within four days. These fish must have been fossilized in less than four days or their gills would not have been preserved.

A man-made hat, a Fedora, was found fossilized after only 40 years on the island of Tasmania. Another hat, a Bowler, was found in New Zealand in 1946. It had fossilized in only 60 years. Next to the Bowler,

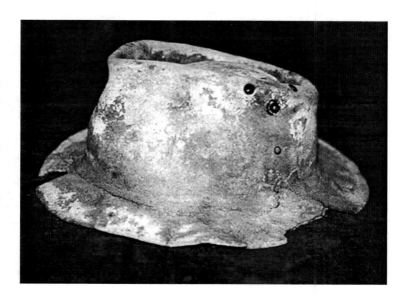

we found a whole ham fossilized. In 1903, at Eureka Springs, Arkansas, we found a bag full of ground flour; the bag and flour were fossilized. Apparently fossilization must be a rapid process.

There is a category of fossilized material known as polystrate fossils. The word poly means "many" and strate refers to "layers." These are fossils which are found to penetrate through two or more layers of the fossil record, meaning that they supposedly existed in two or more of the evolutionary time frames. Polystrate fossils are usually tree trunks, stumps or roots, although they may be bone(s).

We find millions of fossilized tree trunks all over the world which "penetrate" multiple layers of the fossil record. Could these trees have lived for millions of years while these layers formed around them? No. The existence of polystrate fossils shows that the fossil record accumulated very quickly.

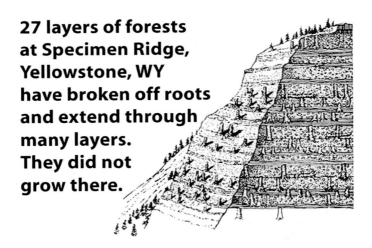

27 layers of forests at Specimen Ridge, Yellowstone, WY have broken off roots and extend through many layers. They did not grow there.

Human artifacts have been found in rock layers dating supposedly as far back as 400 to 500 million years. Over 300 man-made stone tools were found during the California Gold Rush Period (1850 to 1890). They were found in gold bearing gravels and are cataloged at the University of California, Berkeley. The gravels were supposedly 9 to 55 million years old. In 1937, a ceramic spoon was found in a piece of Pennsylvania medium grade coal. In 1889, a fired clay human figurine was discovered in Nampa, Idaho, 320 feet below the surface of the ground, supposedly making this doll 12 million years old. In 1912, in the city of Thomas, Oklahoma, in the middle of a mid-Pennsylvania aged anthracite coal seam, a small black iron pot was found. According to evolutionists, the coal seam was 300 million supposed years old. In Utah, a fossil hunter found the matching top and bottom pieces of a fossil showing a number 9 1/2 man's sandal or moccasin print crushing to death two baby Trilobites.

According to evolutionists, the rock is Cambrian Limestone supposedly 500 to 600 million years ago. Near Glen Rose, Texas, a metal hammer head with a wooden handle attached has been found in a layer of sedimentary rock that evolutionists insist is 400 to 500 million years old.

Sea shells surrounding the hammer had been dated at 400 million years old. Part of the handle had turned to coal.

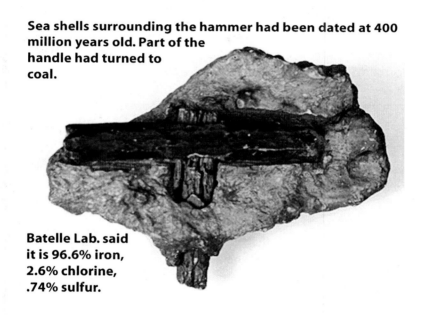

Batelle Lab. said it is 96.6% iron, 2.6% chlorine, .74% sulfur.

These findings clearly refute the claim by evolutionists that humans evolved from apes four million supposed years ago in East Central Africa.

Proof #3—Evolutionists Claim That Homology "Proves" Evolution. Does It?

The study of similar structures is called Homology. The evolutionists claim that random chance has produced similar structures by the inherent ability of matter to achieve optimum design without an outside guiding force. The evolutionists think that the existence of similar structures is caused by common heritage, a common ancestor. The structure of a man's hand, a bat's wing, a whale's flipper and a horse's leg are indeed similar. This would also be expected if creation were true. The study of molecular homology does not show, as so often claimed by the liberal media, a 96 to 99% similarity between the genetic structure of apes and humans. In reality the whole DNA of ape and man is not nearly that close.

According to the prestigious evolutionist magazine Nature, September, 2005, and only considering the genes and not all the intergenic components of the genomes of apes and humans (they are only comparing 3% of the total information in the genomes), there is only an 83% similarity of genes between apes and humans. Even more troublesome for evolutionists, apes only produce 29% the same proteins as humans, while 71% of the proteins are different.

To make matters worse for evolutionists, using "their" chosen method of determining genetic similarity between apes and humans; people are 50% the same as bananas, 88% the same as rats, 60% the same as chickens, and 88% the same as Sea-squirts. Using the evolutionists' chosen method of genetic comparison, who does this make us closer to?

A similar study of Cytochrome C, a universal protein needed for aerobic respiration, clearly shows that every life form is unique, different and unrelated to any other life forms.

The argument from Homology was initially a creationist argument which proponents said that the existence of similar structures showed a common designer not a common ancestry. Designed complex structures and systems do not occur by random chance. When many different engineers are given a design problem and a common goal of finding the "best" design, they will all head in the direction of the same optimum design. Examples of common optimum design are everywhere, for example; cars and ladders.

The similarity of structural appearance between ape and man does not indicate spiritual equivalence. What we do see in nature is a convergence upon a common design. The structural engineering term is "the conservation of engineering design from common desired end function." Apes and men have a similar design probably because God had similar body function in mind. God had perfect designs and He simply used them in many awe-inspiring variations.

Proof #4—Evolutionists Say That Ranking "Proves" Evolution. Does It?

Evolutionists claim that "ranking," the ability to place things in a logical order or sequence by size or shape, proves that evolution is true. Classic illustrations of this technique include the "Horse Series" and "The Road To Man" presentations. The proof method of "ranking," however, is the second worst method of proof in all of science.

The "Horse Series" was thrown out decades ago and no self-respecting evolutionist would claim it to be true today. Eohippus is now classified as a form of Rock Badger. Eohippus and Equus remains have been found within the same sedimentary rock layer, proving that they lived at the same time.

What does ranking prove? If I line up a room full of people using only their height as the guide for where they belong in the line, what have I proven? I have only proved that people come in different heights and that I have the ability and intelligence to arrange them by height. If I line up a room full of people only by their birth month and day only (not year), what have I proven? I have proven that people are born on different days of the year and that I have the ability and intelligence to arrange them by the month and day of their birth.

Ranking proves nothing about the relationship between any two people in either scenario. I have proven nothing about their heritage. I have not proven that any two of them are related in anyway. I have not proven that any one of them is married to another; that any one of them is a mother, father, son or daughter.

The proof by ranking is a useless method of proof. If I place a unicycle next to bicycle next to motorcycle next to an automobile, did I just prove that unicycles evolved into automobiles? If I place a Sand Dollar next to a Frisbee next to a hubcap next to a wheel, did I just prove that Sand Dollars evolved into wheels? No. I have shown that the "Proof by Ranking" is a totally fallacious argument.

I would also caution anyone to be wary of artists' renderings as they are dependent upon the preconceived worldview of the artist. For example, while it was later found out that the fossil tooth from what was initially called Nebraska Man had actually come from an extinct species of pig, a drawing was done in 1922 that showed what Nebraska Man, Nebraska Woman, their clothing and tools looked like. If you give the same skull to two different artists, one believes in evolution and the other in creation, the evolutionist might draw a gorilla, but the creationist might draw a human being.

Proof #5—Evolutionists Claim That Vestigial And Retrogressive Organs And Structures "Prove" Evolution. Do They?

Evolutionists claim that the existence of so-called "vestigial organs," which are those organs that are supposed to be no longer needed because we have evolved past their usefulness, proves that evolution has occurred. The German anatomist Dr. Robert Wiedersheim, in his book *The Structure of Man an Index to His Past History*, 1895, listed 186 (86 vestigial and 100 retrogressive) organs or structures in the human body which were either no longer needed or were atrophying from lack of use. A partial list of the organs and structures he claimed to be vestigial or retrogressive includes: the appendix, the coccyx, the little toes, the parathyroid, the thymus, the pituitary, the pineal and wisdom teeth.

Charles Darwin claimed, in his book *The Origin of Species* (1859 and modified later in 1874), that vestigial organs were essential to the proof for evolution and came either from disuse or natural selection. His premise was that, if a nonfunctional organ was present in a man's body, and was both present and still functional in a monkey's body, it showed that man descended from monkeys. He claimed that vestigial organs demonstrated the atrophying of organs which were no longer needed as they had been bypassed by evolutionary progression.

The creationist points out that the argument that these organs are vestigial, actually stifles scientific and medical research and discovery. Science can only deal with the present and is not able to say anything about the non-existence of a function. To assert that an organ is vestigial is equal to an attempt to prove that no function exists for that organ. The correct scientific statement would be that no function has as yet been observed for a particular organ.

Today, all 186 of the organs or structures present on Wiedersheim's list are known to have one or more specific uses or functions. The first group are those organs which have been incorrectly identified as useless but are now known to have a specific function such as the pineal gland, the pituitary gland and the lachrymal glands. The second group are those organs which are small and have only limited roles such as the wisdom teeth, the small toes and certain veins. The third group are those organs or structures which function only during certain stages in life such as the notochord, the posterior cardinal veins and the ducts of Cuvier. The fourth group are those organs which are developmental "remnants" of the reproductive structures of the opposite sex such as male nipples, male Mullerian ducts and female Wolffian ducts. These structures are not evolutionary remnants; rather **they form prior** to the sexual differentiation that occurs in the development of the human embryo.

If a true vestigial organ or structure did exist, it could show that it was needed and useful at the time of creation; but, that it is either no longer needed, or that it was "switched off" by some genetic change which was triggered by the environmental changes at the time of the Flood of Noah, or that it does not function because of degrading mutations over time (a by-product of the consequences of human sin).

Proof #6—Evolutionists Claim That Embryonic Recapitulation "Proves" Evolution. Does It?

The ardent evolutionist Dr. Ernst Haeckel (1834-1919) was raised to believe in Christianity. But, after reading Darwin's *The Origin of Species* in 1860, he became "Darwin's Bulldog on the Continent."

Haeckel was responsible for inventing several grand frauds. By 1868 many evolutionists were worried about the lack of evidence for Darwin's theory. Haeckel decided to manufacture some evidence. He had begun to draw a "family tree" for mankind. He became worried about the large gap at the bottom between living organisms and non-living materials. To "complete" his chart, he decided to create an entire series of organisms that he called *Moneron* (plural for *Monera*).

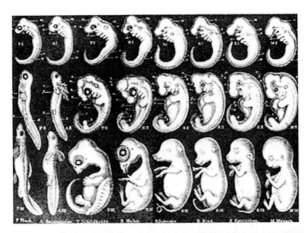

Haeckel's famous (infamous) set of 24 drawings purporting to show eight different embryos in three stages of development, as published by him in *Anthropogenie*, in Germany, 1874.

Haeckel's fake drawings, 1874

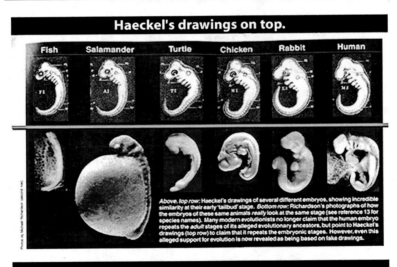

Haeckel's drawings on top.

| Fish | Salamander | Turtle | Chicken | Rabbit | Human |

Above, top row: Haeckel's drawings of several different embryos, showing incredible similarity at their early 'tailbud' stage. Bottom row: Richardson's photographs of how the embryos of these same animals really look at the same stage (see reference 13 for species names). Many modern evolutionists no longer claim that the human embryo repeats the adult stages of its alleged evolutionary ancestors, but point to Haeckel's drawings (top row) to claim that it repeats the embryonic stages. However, even this alleged support for evolution is now revealed as being based on fake drawings.

Actual photos on bottom.

82

These were supposed to be the first single cell organisms to have ever evolved into existence in the supposed primordial sea. He said that they were:

> . . . not composed of any organs at all, but consist entirely of shapeless, simple homogeneous matter . . . nothing more than a shapeless, mobile, little lump of mucus or slime, consisting of albuminous combination of carbon.

In 1868, he published over 30 drawings of these creatures complete with their reproductive cycle illustrated. Dr. Thomas Huxley, M.D., "Darwin's Bulldog in England," claimed to have discovered the creature alive in the sediments of the North Atlantic. Unfortunately for them, in 1875, the chemist, John Buchanan, proved that what Huxley had claimed to have found was nothing more than amorphous gypsum that had precipitated out of sea-water when it had come into contact with the alcohol in the container in which Huxley had placed the sample.

Haeckel refused to admit the fraud and reprinted the fraudulent drawings in the edition of his book *Natural History of Creation* in 1883.

Haeckel's frauds continued with his attempt to prove that the only difference between apes and people was that people could talk. He even went so far as to have an artist, Gabriel Marx, draw the nonexistent ape-man *Pithecanthropus alalus* (speechless ape-man). The evidence for any such creature has never been found, but Haeckel claimed that it was the prehuman that had inhabited Europe.

Haeckel promulgated his most famous fraud called "The Biogenetic Law," or the law of embryonic recapitulation, in his book *Natural History of Creation*, first published in 1868. This idea is often repeated in a summary statement which says, "ontogeny recapitulates (begets) phylogeny." This is the idea that (Ontogeny) the biological development of the individual (recapitulates) repeats briefly (phylogeny) the evolutionary development of the individual.

This false concept proposed that in the womb a human baby passes through the various evolutionary stages of previous life forms and is only born human. His idea was that a human baby starts to develop in a fish stage which then passes through an amphibian stage, then a reptilian stage, then a mammalian stage and is only born human.

In his book, *The Riddle of the Universe at the Close of the Nineteenth Century*, Haeckel wrote:

> When we see that, at a certain stage, the embryos of man and the ape, the dog and the rabbit, the pig and the sheep, though recognizable as higher vertebrates, **cannot be distinguished from each other,** the fact can only be elucidated by assuming a common parentage. [Emphasis added]

Charles Darwin believed his disciple's fraud and continued to claim that the supposed biogenetic law was the single most important evidence for common descent. On page 9 of his book, *The Descent of Man*, Darwin wrote:

> The [human] embryo itself **at a very early period can hardly be distinguished** from that of other members of the vertebrate kingdom. [Emphasis added]

In 1874, Professor Wilhelm His, Sr., uncovered the fraud. Haeckel had stolen the embryonic drawings of two legitimate embryologists, T. L. W. Bischoff (1845) and A. Ecker (1851-1859), and fraudulently changed the drawings to manufacture the evidence for supposed human evolution since he could not support the concept with real anatomical evidence.

In 1875, Haeckel was put on trial by an academic court of his peers at the University of Jena. He was convicted of stealing and lying, and lost his tenured position in the biology department. He confessed:

> . . . a small portion of my embryo-pictures (possibly 6 or 8 in a hundred) are really (in Dr. Brass's [one of his critics] sense of the word) "falsified" — all those, namely, in which the disclosed material for inspection is so incomplete or insufficient that one is compelled in a restoration of a connected development series **to fill up the gaps through hypotheses, and to reconstruct the missing members through comparative syntheses.** What difficulties this task encounters, and how easily the draughtsman may blunder in it, the embryologist alone can judge. [Emphasis added]

I should feel utterly condemned . . . were it not that hundreds of the best observers, and biologists **lie** under the same charge. [Emphasis added]

In 1909, Haeckel admitted his forgery in writing.

In an article published in Science magazine, May 15, 1998, Dr. Michael K. Richardson (an evolutionist), wrote:

The core scientific issue remains unchanged: **Haeckel's drawings of 1874 are substantially fabricated.** In support of this view, I note that his oldest 'fish' image is made up of bits and pieces from different animals - some of them mythical. It is not unreasonable to characterize this as **'faking.'** . . . **Sadly, it is the discredited 1874 drawings that are used in many British and American biology textbooks today.** [Emphasis added]

At the trial in 1875, Haeckel also tried to excuse his actions by saying that spontaneous generation (evolution) was true, not because it had been proven in a laboratory, but because otherwise:

"It would be necessary to believe in a creator." [Emphasis added]

Keith Stewart Thomson wrote "Ontogeny and Phylogeny Recapitulated" for the *American Scientist*, Vol. 76, May-June 1988, p. 273:

"Surely the 'Biogenetic Law' **is as dead as a doornail.**"[Emphasis added]

No evolutionary embryologist would support Haeckel's "Biogenetic Law" as being a law or even being a valid idea. However, the promulgation of Haeckel's fraud has been the justification for many of the evils of this world. His fraud continues to be used by abortionists to convince women that they are only aborting a fish. Adolf Hitler found in Haeckel's fraud the basis for his racism and killed millions using the so-called Biogenetic Law as his justification.

Proof #7—Evolutionists Tell Stories about How Evolution "Could" Have Happened and Claim That These Stories "Prove" Evolution. Do They?

Evolutionists make up pretty stories to try and make their theories sound plausible. Here is one example from Charles Darwin's own writings in an early edition of *The Origin of Species*, 1859, p. 184. This section was removed from later editions after Darwin was criticized by his fellow evolutionists for obvious reasons:

> In North America the black bear was seen by Hearne swimming for hours with widely opened mouth, thus catching, like a whale, insects in the water. Even in so extreme a case as this, if the supply of insects were constant, and if better adapted competitors did not already exist in the country, I can see no difficulty in a race of bears being rendered, by natural selection, more and more aquatic in their structure and habits, with larger and larger mouths, **till a creature was produced as monstrous as a whale.** [Emphasis added]

Such stories were also contrived by Charles Darwin and Thomas Huxley to promote their views in favor of white supremacy, in support of human racism and in justification of their chauvinistic sexism. *In The Descent of Man*, 2nd ed., New York; A. L. Burt Co., 1874, p. 178, Darwin wrote:

> At some future period, not very distant as measured by centuries, the civilized races of man will almost certainly exterminate and replace throughout the world the savage races. At the same time the anthropomorphous apes . . . will no doubt be exterminated. The break will then be rendered wider, for it will intervene between man in a more civilized state, as we may hope, than the Caucasian, and some ape as low as a baboon, **instead of as at present between the negro or Australian and the gorilla.** [Emphasis added]

On page 326, he continued:

> It is generally admitted that with women the powers of

intuition, of rapid perception, and perhaps of imitation, are more strongly marked than in man; but some, at least, of these faculties are characteristic of the lower races, and therefore of a past and lower state of civilization. The chief distinction in the intellectual powers of the two sexes **is shown by man attaining to a higher eminence,** in whatever he takes up, than woman can attain-whether requiring deep thought, reason, or imagination, or merely the use of the senses and hands. [Emphasis added]

In echoing Darwin's sentiments recorded above, Thomas Huxley wrote in his *Lay Sermons, Addresses, and Reviews,* New York: Appleton, 1871 p. 20:

No rational man, cognizant of the facts, believes that **the average negro is the equal, still less the superior, of the white man.** And if this be true, it is simply incredible that, when all his disabilities are removed, and our prognathous relative has a fair field and no favor, as well as no oppressor, he will be able to compete successfully with his bigger-brained and smaller-jawed rival, in a contest which is to be carried on by thoughts and not by bites. [Emphasis added]

Henry Fairfield Osborn was a disciple of Thomas Huxley. He would eventually become the President of the American Museum of Natural History's Board of Trustees from 1908 to 1933. He would continue to strongly promote the evolutionary theories and the racism of his mentor. In an article in the Museum's own magazine, ("The Evolution of Human Races," *Natural History*, April 1980, p. 129—reprinted from January/February 1926 issue) he wrote:

The Negroid stock is even more ancient than the Caucasian and Mongolians, as may be proved by an examination not only of the brain, of the hair, of the bodily characteristics . . . but of the instincts, the intelligence. The standard of **intelligence of the average adult Negro is similar to that of the eleven-year-old-youth of the species *Homo sapiens*.** [Emphasis added]

There are many other such stories which are promulgated by modern evolutionists. The made-up story that the fossil baring layers are in "the right order" thus proving evolution is one. The Geological Time Column or Time Scale is contrived by rearranging the layers found around the world and assembling a mythological column. 75 to 80 percent of the earth's surface is covered by sedimentary rock containing fossils. Yet, 80 to 85 percent of those sedimentary layers do not have even three of the layers shown in the typical school textbook diagram of the Column.

Evolutionists sometimes have a problem swallowing their own stories at times about this myth. Concerning the very method used by evolutionists to "date" their fossil finds, as well as the layers in which they occur, Dr. Niles Eldredge of the American Museum of Natural History drew attention to the problem of circular reasoning used by evolutionists in his book, *Time Frames: The Rethinking of Darwinian Evolution and the Theory of Punctuated Equilibria* New York: Simon and Schuster, 1985, p. 51-52, with the following statement:

"[Evolutionary] Paleontologists cannot operate this way. There is simply no way simply to look at a fossil and say how old it is unless you know the age of the rocks it comes from. . . ."

"And this poses something of a problem: if we date the rocks by their fossils, how can we then turn around and talk about patterns of evolutionary change through time in the fossil record?"

Story-telling can reach its zenith in double-talk. Here is an example from Dr. J. E. O'Rourke writing for the *American Journal of Science*. ("Pragmatism versus Materialism in Stratigraphy," *American Journal of Science*, Vol. 276, January 1976, p. 51.)

> **The rocks do date the fossils, but the fossils date the rocks more accurately.** Stratigraphy cannot avoid this kind of reasoning if it insists on using only temporal concepts, because circularity is inherent in the derivation of time scales. [Emphasis added]

As a final example of story-telling, let us talk about comets. Anyone may check this out for themselves with the aid of a personal computer. Just buy a program on the solar system. The computer will show you where the comets are at any time—past, present or future. We have never found a short-period comet, defined as a comet with an orbit of less than 200 years, that could exist in orbit around the sun for more than about 10,000 years without being destroyed. If the solar system is more than 10,000 years old, then we should no longer have any comets. The few long-period comets that exist would be destroyed in less than 100,000 years.

What is the evolutionary response to this information? The response comes from a Dutch evolutionary astronomer named Dr. Jan Oort who theorized that there "must" be a cloud of pre-comets located one to one and a half light years out from the sun beyond the orbit of Pluto. As comets are being destroyed in the inner solar system, the gravitational pull of the sun then supposedly causes some of these pre-comets to be pulled out of this "cloud" into the solar system, thus producing a continuous stream of new comets to take the place of the old ones which are continuously being destroyed.

The obvious question would be, "Have we seen the supposed Oort Cloud?" No! No confirmed direct observations of the supposed Oort cloud have ever been made. Evolutionary astronomers only believe it to be the source of all comets entering the inner solar system.

It is only a story made up to placate the problem of only having short-period comets in the solar system.

Proof #8—Evolutionists Claim That the Earth and Universe Are Very Old, Thus "Proving" Evolution. Is the Universe Old?

Evolutionists claim that the earth is obviously old and that the fossil materials are the result of slow and gradual accumulation of sedimentary layers over supposed millions and billions of years of time. If this were true, why are there no meteorites found in the sedimentary layers?

Every year about 600 significant meteorites pass through the earth's atmosphere and hit the earth. On average, 30% of them will hit land and be preserved. If the sedimentary layers covering the earth are supposed to represent 600 million years of earth history, we should find 108 billion meteorites in the sedimentary layers.

Wouldn't the lack of meteorites within the fossil materials indicate that the layers all formed during the one year event called Noah's Flood?

Evolutionists claim that the universe is obviously old because it is supposedly 12 to 20 billion light-years in radius, and for light to travel such a distance the universe must be equally old. The major reason for this conclusion is the acceptance of one of the Big Bang "theories" and that any previous explo-sion would cause an expanding universe. The "proof" usually given for accepting an expanding uni-verse is based upon the observed red shift of light, caused by the Doppler Effect.

The idea being that if stars and galaxies are moving away from our solar system due to some Big Bang, then the color of the light they emit will be "stretched" or elongated toward the red "end" of the visible light spectrum. The Doppler Effect would also cause light being emitted from an object moving towards us (there are only a few of those) to be shifted (compressed to a shorter length) towards the blue "end" of the light spectrum.

Most people are "taken in" by this reasoning. However, never confuse distance as measured in light-years as equal to time, it is only a distance! I know of at least eight valid scientific explanations which could, in part or in whole, account for a universe which is 12 to 20 billion light years across and still only be 6,000 years old.

The following is a list of short explanations for the physical evidence of red shift of light as observed in the universe, without having to have the universe expand. I am not endorsing any one of these ideas as being the correct one. There may be truth in any one of these; or a combination of these; or even in another idea which we haven't yet understood, but is actually correct. These explanations are just food for thought until the Creator chooses to reveal the actual truth to us.

1. When God created the Sun, the Moon and the stars He could have simply created all the interconnecting light beams at the same time. Although not totally satisfying, and while it begs many questions, this is a possibility. I definitely do not endorse this view.

2. If Einstein were correct and space is curved, then light could travel across a 12 to 20 billion light-year distance in a matter of a few thousand years.

3. Space is not a true vacuum. As light travels across space it will eventually hit gas or dust particles. When it does, the object will be warmed by radiant heating. The light will then be re-emitted from a warmer object. This in turn will cause the light to be shifted toward the "redder" "end" of the light spectrum. Thus the light will appear to us as though red shift had taken place, when indeed it has not.

4. Einstein also said that light is bent by the force of gravity as it travels by "heavy objects," meaning stars and galaxies. Today, we know he was correct. We have large quantities of photos, many taken by the Hubble astronomy satellite, which clearly show that light is often bent by gravity as it travels through space. Gravity actually acts as a lens (called a Gravitational Lens) and bends light the same way that a glass lens bends visible light. If the speed of light is a constant, when light is bent it must travel a greater distance, and in order to maintain speed it must shift to a "redder" (a longer) wave length; producing a red shift without an expanding universe.

5. A fairly recent idea in science is that perhaps the speed of light is not a true constant, which it is not. Please see the article on our website at www.creationworldview.org concerning the last few decades of research on this subject. The speed of light only appears to be constant today, but has in fact, been faster in the past.

The speed of light has been measured for over 325 years and the data supports such an idea. It all goes back to 1982 in an article written by Dr. Barry Setterfield of Australia entitled "The Velocity of Light and the Age of the Universe." The data indicates that the speed of light could have been nearly infinite in speed less than 10,000 years ago, thus allowing light to traverse a 12 to 20 billion light-year distance in only a few thousand years.

There are evolutionary scientists who agree with this conclusion. In 1987, the Russian theoretical physicist, Dr. V. S. Troitskii working at the Radio-physical Research Institute in Nizhniy Novgorod, Russia, postulated that a huge decay in the speed of light had occurred over time. Dr. Troitskii wrote that the speed of light could have been 10 million times faster in the past compared to what it is today. His work is found in the British journal *Astrophysics and Space Science* 139 (1987) 389-411 "Physical Constants and Evolution of the Universe."

In addition, since 1999 experiments have been conducted by evolution believing physicists in Holland, Germany, Australia, and the United States (Texas A&M, Princeton and Harvard) demonstrating that light can be accelerated, decelerated and even stopped and started again. Light speed is not a constant and a light-year is at best a variable yardstick and at worse a useless yardstick.

6. Dr. Russell Humphreys has recently proposed that the solution is found by using Relativity Theory and the Scripture. Although too complex for this short explanation, he proposes that since the creation, the universe has experienced "Gravitational Time Dilation." While this idea will be argued for a long time to come, many of his ideas are sound in concept and could help to explain why we have a universe that is only 6,000 years old, but appears to be 12 to 20 billion light-years across.

7. The Second Law of Thermodynamics stipulates that all physical entities spontaneously degrade over time. Why should light be the only physical entity in the entire university that would be exempt from the Second Law? It cannot be exempt! Light is subject to the effect of the Second Law; therefore, light speed must diminish over time. This would cause light to "slow down" in its frequency, which, in turn, would appear to us as red shift even though no red shift has occurred.

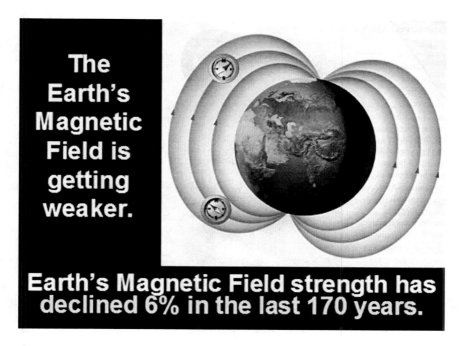

The Earth's Magnetic Field is getting weaker.

Earth's Magnetic Field strength has declined 6% in the last 170 years.

8. The Law of Gravity affects every location in the universe. There is no such thing as "zero gravity." Even in the most remote spot in the universe microgravity still exists. It is not a question of whether gravity exists at any one place; it is only a question of how much gravity exists at any one place.

Everyone knows that the speed of light differs depending upon the medium that it is traveling through, i.e., light travels slightly slower through water than through air or a vacuum. As light travels through the universe it passes through areas that have much higher and much lower concentrations of gravity, i.e., gravity is less dense between galaxies, much denser inside galaxies and very dense inside solar systems.

We are only able to measure the speed of light inside our solar system. We are not able to measure it between stars, solar systems, galaxies nor throughout the universe. Light speed should be faster in areas of lower gravity density and slower when passing through areas of higher gravity density. We may think of this as areas of more or less resistance.

Consequently, the speed of light would have been much faster initially as it began to cross the universe, but would be slowing down over time. Finally, it would slow to the speed that we perceive it here and now.

Evolutionary claims that the universe and all it contains are old go on and on. The truth is that such claims are unsubstantiated.

There is not one irrefutable piece of evidence to "prove" that the earth and universe are old. There are no reliable radiometric dating technologies. Carbon 14, Potassium-Argon, Rubidium-Strontium, etc. do not work! These highly relied upon methods start with five false assumptions, and Carbon 14 starts with seven false assumptions. They are totally unreliable.

Paleontology is no help to evolutionists. You cannot date the fossils based upon the sedimentary rock layers that they were found in; and then turn around and date the layers based upon the fossils that they contain. The claims of great age are based solely upon the evolutionists' belief system.

There are over 200 scientific Geochronometers (earth time clocks/universe time clocks) that indicate that the earth, solar system, galaxy and universe are young, much too young for evolution to be a possibility. A few examples of these are as follows:

1. The rapid decay of the earth's magnetic field

2. The existence of high pressure natural gas contained within sedimentary (porous) rock layers

3. The existence of Short-period Comets

4. The rapid heat loss of the earth and moon

5. The rapid recession rate of the moon

6. The "lumpy" rings of Saturn and Uranus

7. The existence of Barred Spiral Galaxies

8. The rapid continental erosion rates

9. The salt content of the oceans

10. There is too much Helium contained within the earth's crustal rocks

11. The accumulation of about 4,500 years of sediments at the mouths of all major rivers

12. The active volcanoes on Jupiter's moon Io, and Saturn's moon Enceladus

13. The existence of Thorium 230 and Uranium 236 on the surface of the moon

14. The annual addition on average of one cubic mile of Juvenile Water to the earth's surface

15. Fresh dinosaur blood and flesh have been found inside T. rex bones

16. There are far too few Supernovas in the universe

17. The existence of millions of tightly folded unbroken sedimentary rock layers around the world

18. The absence of meteorites in the sedimentary rock layers containing fossils

19. The lack of Helium in the earth's atmosphere

20. The rapid growth of stalactites and stalagmites

21. The lack of soil horizons between sedimentary rock layers

22. The lack of V-shaped erosion marks in sedimentary rock layers

23. The lack of animal and plant burrows in sedimentary rock layers

24. The existence of billions of polystrate fossils in the sedimentary rock layers

25. "The Winding Up Dilemma"—galaxies rotate too fast to be billions of years old

If there were only one Geochronometer showing that the earth or universe were young, then it could be claimed that creationists are wrong. If there were several Geochronometers that show that the earth and universe are young, then we would have established an interesting trend. When there are over 200 Geochronometers that are in agreement; that the earth, solar system, galaxy and universe are young; then we have substantial "proof" contrary to the opinion of evolutionists.

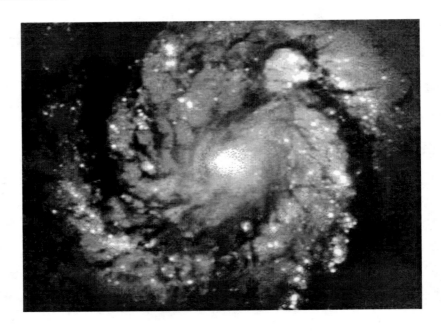

Proof #9—Evolutionists Claim That Genetic Studies "Prove" Evolution. Do They?

Evolutionists claim that the study of genetics demonstrates the mechanism by which progressive "upward" macroevolution takes place. The Laws of Genetics, however, are conservative, not creative. No evolutionary believing scientist may speak and have evolution occur at his beckoned command; nor have we ever seen an evolutionary believing scientist speak and see a new gene appear at the bottom of a test tube.

What does the creationist claim? Modern genetic research has shown that there is even a repair mechanism within the genetic materials to repair slightly damaged information and take corrective measures to combat mutational copying errors. Anything less than a perfect copy proves, in the long run, to be less fit rather than more fit for survival.

It takes phenomenal faith to believe that the DNA molecule could come into existence by random chance. How much more faith does it take to believe that a corrective mechanism to the first randomly generated mechanism could arise by random chance?

What if we were to spend billions of dollars and utilize many millions of man hours and finally "create life" in a test tube; what would we have proven? We would have proven that it takes a great amount of outside intelligence; massive amounts of information and energy; an ordering process to "create life;" and, that it did not happen by random chance.

Proof #10 (?)—The "Tenth" Proof?: Evolutionists Claim That the Imperfection of Nature Proves Evolution. Does It?

There is a new "tenth proof" for evolution that is being fostered by some evolutionists. Although it is not being widely supported, it is accepted by several very prominent personalities in the field of evolutionary theorists.

The new "proof" goes like this: plants and animals are not perfect, they contain imperfections; a perfect creator would make things that are perfect; therefore, the existence of life that is imperfect shows that there was no creator.

The main proponent of this idea was the late Marxist from Harvard, Dr. Stephen J. Gould. In an article for *Discover* magazine in May, 1981, he wrote:

> The second argument—that the imperfection of nature reveals evolution—strikes many people as ironic, for they feel that evolution should be most elegantly displayed in the nearly perfect adaptation expressed by some organisms—the camber of a gull's wing, or butterflies that cannot be seen in ground litter because they mimic leaves so precisely. But perfection could be imposed by a wise creator or evolved by natural selection. Perfection covers the tracks of past history. And past history—the evidence of descent—is the mark of evolution. **Evolution lies exposed in the imperfections that record a history of descent.** [Emphasis added]

Dr. Gould then attached this "proof from imperfection" to the argument from Homology. Homology may be defined as: similar structures among creatures are evidence that they had a common ancestor with the same feature. Homology is actually evidence that the Creator chose to use similar structures to achieve similar results.

Gould continued in his *Discover* article:

"Why should a rat run, a bat fly, a porpoise swim, and I type this essay with structures built of the same bones unless we all inherited them from a common ancestor? An engineer, starting from scratch, could design better limbs in each case."

This is a great faith statement. The logic is most peculiar and convoluted. Evolutionists have dogmatically believed that the mechanisms of natural selection, survival of the fittest, Uniformitarianism, etc., were causing life forms to irreversibly evolve in an "upward" progression. Now, evolutionists would want us to believe that you can have your cake and eat it, too. They want to blame the imperfections of life upon the nonexistence of a creator rather than upon the happenstance of random chance.

It is impossible for evolutionists to make such dogmatic statements about things that are "perfect" or "imperfect." How would a human being know if something were perfect? We have no basis, no standard, by which to make such a claim. We strive for "optimum" designs, but we are incapable of knowing if we have achieved them. Even if we derive mathematical constraints they were subjectively derived. Ultimately, "perfect" and "optimum" for a human design is subjective and nothing more than opinion.

A "perfect" creation is one that completely fulfills the purpose of its creator. Dr. Gould could not create a living cell, much less a rat's forelimb. Furthermore, he was totally ignorant of the global, cosmic and eternal purposes of the Creation. Therefore, Gould's opinion about how they should have been designed was hopelessly arrogant, ignorant and irrelevant.

There are lots of complex structures, these structures contain many similarities, they are clearly well designed, yet evolutionists claim that they show evidence of less than perfect design. Since all the complex systems whose origin we have observed were created by intelligent agents (human beings), since they contain countless similar structures, and are virtually all "imperfect," the best, most scientific, explanation of complex structures whose origin we have not observed, e.g., the forelimbs of rats, the wings of bats, is that they, too, were created by an intelligent agent. Appeal to random processes as an agent is not even remotely supported by the present data.

Every "proof" of evolution involves willful deception, just as the Bible says it will. Evolutionists are not ignorant that the Bible records God saying that He cursed "all the creation" in Genesis 3. Paul called it "the bondage to decay" in Romans 8:21. These verses provide us with a perfectly plausible Biblical explanation for "imperfection." "Imperfection" cannot possibly be a proof of evolution when it is also a proof of the Bible.

In the same way, evolutionists will speak of "convergence," the supposed reason that explains why some creatures have very similar structures but cannot be directly related (wings for insects and mammals). Evolutionists use "convergence" when they cannot fit things on their tree of evolutionary ascent. Homology only proves evolution if it were to come from common ancestry, but when it cannot you call it "convergence" by natural selection toward an "optimum" design. Evolutionists want it both ways and they pick the one that suites them at the time.

We have never seen a complex system built or assembled by random chance. Mutations are harmful and produce negative outcomes. Mutations are the result of the "bondage to decay." The evolutionists' beliefs are illogical, irrational, unreasonable and not based on evidence.

The evolutionist is missing the point of what is the better substantiated view of the known data. The correct view would be that the Creator did in fact make all things perfect, but that something happened after the creation; sin entered into the universe. This event brought imperfection into the creation and like a snowball rolling downhill imperfection has continuously gotten worse.

Every "Proof" of evolution involves willful deception, just as God says it will. There is hope, for we are told that there will come a time when the Creator will enter into human history and restore imperfection back to perfection once again (2 Peter 3:3-7).

PEOPLE LIVED TO BE 900 YEARS OLD?

The Bible records that people used to live to a vast number of years of age as compared to the present day human life expectancy. The average age of the patriarchs from creation to the Flood, excluding Enoch and Lamech, was 912 years old. Are there scientific and medical explanations which would support these statements of great age or are they mythological? **Yes**, there is data from both the scientific and the medical fields to support these statements.

If we look at the age at which the various patriarchs died as recorded in the Book of Genesis, we see that there is a clearly defined downward turning exponential curve associated with the decreasing ages of mankind. From creation to the Flood, everyone lived about the same number of years. After the Flood, the life expectancy dropped rapidly as the outside environment and internal body mechanisms degraded over time. Here are samples of seven scientific and twelve medical reasons that caused this to happen. (The following are only a partial listing of reasons and should not be considered an exhaustive listing.)

What Scientific Reasons Are There to Believe in a 900 Year Life Expectancy?

Genetics

People started out with perfect genetic material at the time of creation. This genetic material remained perfect until the time shortly after creation when mankind sinned. This event brought imperfection into the universe. The mechanism which continues this process of becoming more and more imperfect is called the Second Law of Thermodynamics in science, and it is a part of "The Curse" of Genesis

3:17, Romans 8:20-22 and Revelation 33:3.

The Second Law of Thermodynamics applies to all natural and physical systems, including biological ones. The Second Law also applies to the transfer of information, and in this special case, use of the concept which is called Information Theory. Information Theory says that every time you handle information, some of it will be lost and that no new organized information will spontaneously arise.

Today, we know that one of the major reasons people no longer live to be 900 years old is that their genetic information has been degraded by the accumulation of mutational copying errors over time. The aging process is accomplished, in part, by the breakdown of the chromosomal information inside the cells of your body.

Magnetic Field of the Earth

The strong magnetic field of the earth during the first few thousand years of earth history would have had two major influences upon human longevity in the past.

The decline of the earth's magnetic field has been measured scientifically since 1835. Based upon this information we may determine that the field was substantially stronger in the past. The magnetic field would have been ten times stronger than it is now at the time of the Flood, about 4,500 years ago. It would have been twenty times stronger at the time of creation, about 6,000 years ago. Laboratory experiments conducted on animals by Dr. Jeno Barnothy in the 1960's have shown that exposure to intense magnetism from the time of conception to the time of puberty stabilizes their chromosomes, slows their aging process and increases their longevity.

The earth's magnetic field has a second influence upon longevity. The magnetic field of the earth holds in place the three Van Allen Radiation Belts which surround the earth. If the magnetic field is stronger, these Belts are held further away from the surface; conversely, if the field weakens, these Belts would descend closer and closer to the earth's surface. Since the earth's magnetic field was stronger in the past, this would have kept these Belts farther away from the earth and obviously lowered the effect of radiation upon all life-forms on the surface.

Today, we know that as the field weakens, we are exposed to more and more radiation which speeds up the aging process and causes a demonstrable rise in cancer cases.

Weather

The Bible tells us that at the time of creation there was far more moisture contained in the earth's atmosphere than there is now. This blanket of moisture was dissipated at the time of the Flood, but it would have provided for longevity in two ways.

First, it would have provided for an environment something like a greenhouse all over the earth. That would have meant that there would have been relatively uniform temperatures all over the earth, even from pole to pole. Wind is produced by a temperature gradient. Basically, on the surface of the earth, wind may be defined as the movement of cold air towards places where warm air is rising. Since the temperatures on the surface prior to the Flood would have been relatively uniform, there would have been little temperature gradient, and therefore, little wind. Prior to the Flood no one would have died from being subjected to strong violent weather patterns or severe seasonal weather patterns. There were simply no hurricanes, tornadoes, thunderstorms or lightning which would have killed people prior to the Flood. In fact, there was no rain prior to the start of the Flood.

Second, the high moisture content of the atmosphere would have also acted as an umbrella to block out much of the incoming ultraviolet (UV) radiation. Exposure to UV radiation has a direct effect upon skin cancers, cataracts and certain other diseases.

Today, we are exposed to much higher levels of UV radiation than the people living prior to the Flood and we have the well-documented rise in cancers to prove it.

Volcanoes and Earthquakes

The Bible describes that there was no appreciable amount of earthquake activity, nor the volcanic activity which frequently accompanies it, from creation to the Flood. The first time these things are mentioned is at the beginning of the Flood. The start of the Flood is described as a time when the earth was massively "cleaved" from below, breaking up the earth's crust, and releasing huge quantities of hot water which were stored below the surface. When hot liquid water came up from below, hot liquid rock came up with it. This, in turn, caused tens of thousands of volcanoes to erupt all over the earth.

The lack of such earthquake and volcanic activity prior to the Flood would have contributed to human longevity. Today, thousands of people may die in just one earthquake or volcanic eruption. Consider what would happen if thousands of earthquakes and volcanic eruptions were to all occur at the same time.

Pollution

From the time of creation to the Flood there was little natural or man-made pollution. The major industry of mankind prior to the Flood was agriculture. The agricultural work was accomplished by the work of people and animals, not tractors and combines. The heavy industry described as existing prior to the Flood, such as the smelting of metallic ores, was relatively insignificant. The first significant pollution to occur after creation was when hundreds of cubic kilometers of volcanic ash were released at the initiation of the Flood.

Today, pollution of the environment is an important topic of discussion, although it is highly misstated in the press and highly misunderstood by the public at large. Fifty years ago, people were being told that the solution to pollution was dilution. We know that is simply not true. The solution to pollution is prevention as we shall explore in the last chapter of the book.

What Medical Reasons Are There to Believe in a 900 Year Life Expectancy?

Food

In Genesis Chapter One, God instructed Adam and Eve to eat of the green plants; they were to be **as** meat to their bodies. First, we see that from creation to the Flood, people and animals were all vegetarians. It was only after the Flood that God issued a new directive to Noah and his family that things had changed, and now they were going to have to eat animal flesh as well as vegetable material in order to survive. Second, apparently while plant products had provided all the necessary nutrients and amino acids for life prior to the Flood, the continuing ravages from the degrading of genetic information and the downhill slide of the environment had taken its toll and plants were no longer able to do so after the Flood.

Today, the health benefits to be derived from a diet high in vegetable matter and low in animal fat are well known. Such a diet would prevent most heart and artery disease, prevent most high blood pressure problems and promote general good health. Caution should be taken, however, in advocating an all-vegetable diet. God said that we were to eat both vegetables and meat; that we were to eat them in proper proportions; and that we were to eat them in moderation.

The Waters Above

At the beginning God created the earth with high moisture content in the earth's atmosphere, part of "the waters above" as described in Genesis. The extra weight of this volume of water suspended in the air caused the atmosphere to weigh 2.0 to 2.2 times the current amount. Living on the earth prior to the Flood would have been like living in a hyperbaric chamber. This added pressure caused the oxygen content in the blood of living organisms to be doubled, which in turn led to the large size of plants and animals and to the rapid healing of wounds. What might have been a lethal injury after the Flood was not a lethal injury prior to the Flood. This would have promoted longevity.

Today, some modern hospitals are equipped with hyperbaric chambers because certain types of wounds heal much faster when they are exposed to high oxygen concentrations. Certainly rapid healing from injuries prior to the Flood would increase the average life span.

The high moisture content of the atmosphere prior to the Flood would have also protected life on earth from some of the harmful radiation coming in from cosmic rays and x-rays that are now bombarding earth. The forty days and forty nights of rain brought this moisture barrier down and the present forces in nature are unable to regenerate it.

Stress

Many people today try to downplay the damaging role stress plays in our daily lives. Today, its effects are well documented, but prior to the Flood there was much less stress. This was because, while work was required to get food, shelter and clothing; food, shelter and clothing were easily supplied. The conditions which existed prior to the Flood allowed for plant crops to grow year around. So while there was effort involved in survival, the level of stress was much lower.

Stress was lower for several other reasons as well. There was no stress from high population densities as there was ample land available for all. Attack by wild animals was not a threat to human life since all the animals were vegetarian. The earth was a veritable green house and crops could be planted immediately after the harvest of the prior crop. The water needs of crops was automatically taken care of, so the building of irrigation systems was unnecessary. In essence, God provided an abundance of all the things necessary for life and so the level of stress was minimal, promoting long life.

Immune System

The human immune system was originally created perfect and this would most certainly have increased life expectancy. Our immune system did not start off with the accumulation of genetic errors which have now made it less effective. The initial immune system of people might have been able to fend off many, if not all, of the diseases which are now common among the human population.

Initially, there would have been no genetic diseases. Hemophilia would not have existed. The "load" of genetic mutations which makes it disastrous for near relatives to intermarry did not built up sufficiently to be a problem until the time of Moses, a period of 1,000 years after the Flood. Even Abraham married his own half-sister without a problem, and their offspring is in the messianic line. By the time of Moses, however, God had to step in and command that there be no more close marriages. The need for genetic diversity to combat genetic disease had come to fruition.

Natural Pharmaceuticals

If evolution were true, we would expect to see more and more species of plants and animals evolving into existence. The opposite, however, is true, which is at least an indicator that creation is also true. Every year species are becoming extinct and no new ones are coming into being. We cannot know what medicinal value or beneficial nutrients might have been available to people from plants which are now extinct. We know of many plant species which are extinct, but we can only speculate what benefits they might have passed on to us. Plant life, both living and extinct, may have contained chemicals, vitamins, nutrients and immunity drugs, of which we are not even aware today.

This is a two-edged sword. The coincident degrading of the human genetic information over time may mean that we are no longer able to utilize the food we eat in order to live as healthy a life as the people did prior to the Flood. We are not able to know what changes have occurred in us over time which may have lessened our ability to digest or utilize food and the food we eat is not as nutritious as it once was. Both edges mean that we will not live as long as humans were once able to live.

Exercise

The people of the pre-Flood world led, for the most part, an agrarian life style. Even in the "cities," the people would have, in general, led a more vigorous lifestyle than we lead today. The agrarian lifestyle with its aerobic physical demands would have been much more healthy than our current sedentary lifestyle. Physical fitness and good nutrition would have been the rule of the day.

Conclusion

These scientific and medical factors, combined with others, show how men could have indeed lived for hundreds of years, even 900 years!

ENVIRONMENTAL ISSUES AND THE CHRISTIAN

God made man and woman. God gave them the mandates of dominion and stewardship over the earth. Today, "Environmental Terrorists" are attempting to convince everyone that unless we abandon our cars and stop further economic growth, we will all perish and the earth with us. Are environmental terrorists to be believed? Is the earth heating up? Is there an "Ozone Hole?" Is "Global Warming" true? Do we need to lock away all our natural resources so as not to allow "those mean capitalists" to get their greedy little hands on them? Is the Green Movement truly concerned about the environment, or is it just the new home of Communism and Socialism? What are the correct Christian responses to all these allegations? Should Christians be preservationists **or** conservationists?

Exactly What Did God Give Man When He Gave the Mandates of Dominion and Stewardship?

Dominion may be termed a "Creation Ordinance" or a creation command. The word translated "dominion" (Hebrew *radah*) means: "to have dominion, to rule, to have authority over, to subjugate, to administer, to take care of and to have superintendence." It does not mean: to rule with an iron fist, to lord it over in a tyrannical manner, to needlessly destroy, nor to exploit.

The word "dominion" as it is used in Genesis means to exercise dominion under God's supervision; following God's direction and example. For example, God states that the principle of the Sabbath rest is to be extended to all areas of His creation. In Leviticus 25:1-7, the Sabbath rest applies to the earth and the agricultural land. In Deuteronomy 25:4, the Sabbath rest applies to the animals. In Exodus 20:8-11, the Sabbath rest applies to mankind.

Profit

Our God is a God of profit. The word "profit," as I use it here, does not refer to money. God doesn't need money; He owns everything. The word "profit," as used in this chapter, means "a return for effort." God expects "a return for effort." The Bible tells us that God's Word will not return void. Every parable concerning the distribution of talents to stewards expected some return for the investment. Each steward was not expected to earn the same amount of return, but each steward was expected to be faithful and earn some "profit." God abhors exploitation or profit for profit's sake. "Profit" is to be for the glory of God and the good of His creation. The dominion mandate provides for the derivation of benefit while also being consistent with the second major biblical principle, that of stewardship.

Stewardship

What is a "steward?" A steward is one who is paid to manage the estate or property belonging to another. A steward is one who is held accountable for his wise or unwise management of that property by the owner. Who is the Owner? According to Psalm 24:1, "The earth is the Lord's, and all it contains, the world, and those who dwell in it." Stewardship then is the act of being a steward accountable to God, and God expects us to be good stewards (2 Corinthians 5:9 and Psalms 8:6).

Stewardship, however, is not preservation; it is positive purposeful management (Ecclesiastes 3:1-8). Even Christ's death on the cross, a destructive act if only looked at on the surface, was required in order to usher in redemption. Stewardship is purposeful both now and in the future. It avoids the short term quick fix which yields long term disaster. An example would be the previous widespread sale and use of DDT without the consideration of the long term effects upon the worldwide environment.

Stewardship requires industry and toil (Genesis 2:15). Man was to work in the Garden of Eden and care for it. When God put Adam in the Garden, He made him the head horticulturist in charge of it. God illustrated industriousness by planting the Garden and working six days during the Creation Week to give us an example; these were His patterns of how we are to live our lives.

Stewardship incorporates preventive maintenance and routine maintenance. Preventive maintenance is making sure that we do not intentionally put long-term toxic chemicals into our world. Routine maintenance is the task of keeping balances between providing for human needs and the short term abuse or exploitation of our God-given resources. Immunization from disease is a good example of maintenance. No one would argue that immunization against the spread of infectious diseases isn't a good idea. Likewise, the reforestation of trees after timber harvest is wise maintenance.

Stewardship includes the prevention of waste. God condemns haste and waste (Proverbs 6:6-11 and Matthews 25:26). In 1960, the schools were teaching that "The Solution to Pollution is Dilution." In God's perspective "The Solution to Pollution is Prevention." Waste usually results from bad management and irresponsibility, and ultimately, directly from sin. God does not waste a single thing (Romans 8:28 and Ephesians 1:11). Prevention of waste requires hard work and energy. The prevention of waste, the minimizing of waste and the recycling of waste requires effort.

Stewardship is personal. Our one and only absolute responsibility is to be faithful (1 Corinthians 4:2). We are to be faithful regardless of the amount with which we are entrusted (Matthews 25:14-30). We are to be faithful with all that we have been entrusted (Romans 14:10-12, 2 Corinthians 5:9-10 and 1 Corinthians 3:12-14). Our reward is not based on the quantity of our profit, but upon our faithfulness, commitment and diligence in handling what we have been given to steward.

There are four benefits that a person receives for faithful stewardship. First, we receive a more intimate relationship with Jesus Christ (Matthews 25:21). Second, it develops our character. Third, by understanding our position as stewards, we may develop true contentment. Fourth, faithful stewardship yields financial order in our families' long term economic stability. On the other hand, the consequences of unfaithful stewardship are to be found in Luke 16:1-15.

How can we develop our minds in the area of good stewardship, or any other area of life for that matter? This can be accomplished by working through the outline below:

1. We condition our minds, in this case, with the Word of God.

2. This leads to mental assent; we are to think in obedience to God.

3. We make a decision to change our thoughts to His thoughts.

4. Through repeated thought, we form a habit.

5. Through regular habit, we develop a pattern of thought.

6. From a pattern of thought, we develop an attitude.

7. From an attitude, we develop a consistent set of actions.

8. Our consistent actions become our firm behavior.

Are the Environmental Terrorists Correct about the Various Environmental Issues?

The "Ozone Hole"

Is there an "Ozone Hole" over southern South America created by man-made air pollution? No. There is no "hole" in the atmosphere; there is only a thinning, depletion, or "dip" in the upper atmosphere which occurs every spring in the Antarctic and is filled back in after about six to ten weeks. Ozone is made in the upper atmosphere by sunlight providing the energy to combine three normal oxygen (3 x O_2) molecules into two ozone (2 x O_3) molecules. This production process occurs 24 hours per day around the world.

The loss of some ozone has been happening every spring over southern South America for hundreds, if not thousands, of years. It is caused when the concentration of chlorofluorocarbons (CFCs or Freon), bromine, chlorine and fluorine builds up in the atmosphere during the cold Antarctic polar night. In the Antarctic spring, the warmth of the sun returning to the southern hemisphere starts a chemical reaction in which these chemicals and ozone combine, destroying

112

large quantities of ozone. After about six to ten weeks, this "depletion" is filled back in through the natural production processes described above and the problem is resolved until the next year.

The great fear that ozone depletion brings with it is that without ozone we are unprotected from the very harmful ultra-violet (UV) radiation that comes to us from the sun. Without ozone, we would most assuredly die. Therefore, it would be critical to the world if ozone levels did reach zero.

Recent research shows, however, that UV radiation levels around the world have dropped not increased, in recent years. Surprisingly, this drop has been due to the "protective layer" of industrial wastes in the atmosphere, in the form of sulfur dioxide and various aerosols, which have been added to the atmosphere by man. These industrial wastes have caused sunlight to bounce off the top of the layer back into outer space and have caused the earth below to cool.

Besides, Freon and other CFCs, bromine, chlorine and fluorine are also made by nature, not just by men and women. These chemicals are produced by macro-algae (marine invertebrates) and volcanoes. Up to 80% of these chemicals are manufactured by volcanoes. Can you legislate against a volcano? Would you like to guess where one of the world's largest air polluting volcanoes is? Right! It is under the "Ozone Hole" at the south end of Chile. Do you think that there could be any coincidence?

It is estimated that we are going to spend One Trillion Dollars to prevent ozone depletion. All that expense is for nothing, except to placate the consciences of environmental terrorists! Is it worth spending One Trillion Dollars to prevent only 20% of the entire world's production of ozone depleting chemicals?

Global Warming? Absolutely No Truth To It!

Is the earth heating up? Are we all going to die from this heat, causing the world to become a large desert? If we don't stop using our cars, will we as a society survive the coming holocaust? What is the truth?

Our awesome Creator God has much to say in the Bible about global weather and climate change from the time of creation, 6,000 years ago, to the present time, and even in the future. Many Christians have failed to think of these Scriptures when trying to evaluate whether or not they should be concerned about these issues. In addition, there is a massive amount of solid science that refutes any claim that "Global Warming" or that "Global Cooling" are true.

God promises that the earth cannot and will not be destroyed by Man [Genesis 8:22]

The promotion of "Global Warming" is purely a political agenda of the Far-Left. **These people may be accurately classified as Environmental Terrorists.** "Global Warming" is believed in even though such a belief is irrational. Note this quote attributed to the former Democratic Senator from Colorado, Tim Wirth:

> We've got to ride the global warming issue. **Even if the theory is wrong, we will be doing the right thing**—in terms of economic policy and the environmental policy." [Emphasis added] (Fumento, Michael, *Science Under Siege*, 1993)

Further proof of the twisted philosophical reasoning of Environmental Terrorists is provided by "Global Warming" advocate Dr. Stephen Schneider. He is Professor, Department of Biological Sciences; Senior Fellow, Stanford Institute for International Studies; Co-Director, Center for Environmental Science and Policy; Co-Director, Interdisciplinary Program in Environment and Resources Stanford University; and, founder and editor of the journal *Climate Change*. In the October, 1989 issue of *Discover* magazine, he wrote:

> On the one hand, as scientists we are ethically bound to the scientific method, **in effect promising to tell the truth, the whole truth, and nothing but**—which means that we must include all doubts, the caveats, the ifs, ands and buts. On the other hand, we are not just scientists but human beings as well. And like most people we'd like to see the world a better place, which in this context translates into our working to reduce the risk of potentially disastrous climate change. To do that we

need to get some broad based support, **to capture the public's imagination.** That, of course, means getting loads of media coverage. So **we have to offer up scary scenarios, make simplified, dramatic statements, and make little mention of any doubts we might have.** This 'double ethical bind' we frequently find ourselves in cannot be solved by any formula. Each of us has to decide what **the right balance is between being effective and being honest.** I hope that means being both.

He wants to be both effective and honest, a noble goal; however, when it comes to promoting "Global Warming" he is quite willing to **"offer up scary scenarios, make simplified, dramatic statements, and make little mention of any doubts we might have."**

This chapter could be filled with just such quotes, but space does not allow this. Thus, as a third and final example of the mental state of the current "crop" of Environmental Terrorists, I submit this **irrational, illogical, unreasonable and unscientific statement** by one of the "head gurus" of Environmental Terrorism, none other than Mr. Al Gore:

> We are dumping so much carbon dioxide into the Earth's environment that **we have literally changed the relationship between the Earth and the Sun.** [Emphasis added] The Introduction to *An Inconvenient Truth*, 2006

God promises that the earth cannot and will not be destroyed by Man [Psalm 148:5-6]

Is "Global Warming" True?

No! We are simply experiencing normal weather and climate fluctuations.

We are living at the end of the **"20th Century Warm Period."** The "20th Century Warm Period" followed a time called **"The Little Ice Age"** that lasted from approximately **1250-1300 through 1850-1900.** Prior to "The Little Ice Age," the earth experienced a period referred to as the **"Medieval Warm Period"** or **"Medieval Climate Optimum."** The earth was significantly warmer during that period than it is today!

Even evolutionary climatologists have proven scientifically that the earth has experienced **three periods of time much warmer than** today's warm period. The various periods of warm and cold, that have been named, have been determined to be approximately:

The Minoan Warm Period - 1450 to 1250 BC

The Roman Warm Period - 250 BC to AD 1

The Dark Ages Cold Period - AD 1 to 800

The Medieval Warm Period - AD 800 to 1250

The Little Ice Age - AD 1250 to 1900

The 20th Century Warm Period - AD 1900 to 2010

Source: Grootes, P.M. (et. al.), "Comparison of oxygen isotope records from the GISP2 and GRIP Greenland ice cores," *Nature*, 366 1993, pp. 552-4.

What is the historical evidence?

We have significant historical evidence with which to trace the major fluctuations in climate change over the past few millennia. These sources include, but are not limited to:

The thousands of years of records of the Nile floods

The 1st-century Roman wine production in England

The thousands of museum paintings that portray sunnier skies during the Medieval Warm Period

The thousands of museum paintings that portray the cloudier skies during the Little Ice Age

The physical evidence from oxygen isotopes, beryllium ions, tiny sea and pollen fossils, ancient tree rings, polar ice cores, sea and lake sediments, cave stalactites and stalagmites, glaciers, etc.

These and many other sources illustrate that the earth has had periods of climate much warmer than today.

God promises that Man cannot change the weather [Ecclesiastes 1:5-10].

Is there scientific consensus that "Global Warming" is true?

NO! Consensus is not the same as truth. Consensus is not data; it is not the same as a scientific fact.

NO! Dr. Richard Lindzen, Alfred P. Sloan Professor of Meteorology at MIT, former lead author of the United Nations International Panel on Climate Change (UN IPCC), wrote about global warming: **". . . the consensus was reached before the research had begun."**

NO! The current promotion of the global warming scare is **purely a far left political agenda.**

NO! "Global Warming" is simply the new home of socialism and communism.

NO! The earth's temperature has been fluctuating up and down for thousands of years because of well established and documented variations in solar activity. These are:

The Schwabe Cycle: Sunspot activity follows an eleven year cycle that causes the sun's temperature to fluctuate up and down 0.1%.

The Gleissberg Cycle: A cycle every 75 to 90 years.

The Suess Cycle: A cycle every 200 to 500 years.

The Bond Cycle: A cycle every 1,100 to 1,500 years.

NO! Dr. Timothy Patterson, Canadian geologist, wrote in the Canadian Financial Post, June 20, 2007: "Climate stability has never been a feature of planet earth. The only constant about climate is change; it changes and, at times, quite rapidly. Many times in the past, temperatures were far higher than today, and occasionally, temperatures were lower."

NO! Dr. Bert Bolin, Swedish meteorologist, for eight years the Chairman of the UN IPCC, noted: "The climate issue is not 'settled'; it is both uncertain and incomplete."

NO! Dr. Dennis Bray, Emeritus Professor, Department of Physiology, University of Cambridge, submitted the following to *Science* for publication on December 22, 2004 (but not accepted): "The most recent survey [2004] of climate scientists . . . found that while there had been a move towards acceptance of [man-made] global warming, **only 9.4% of respondents 'strongly agree'** that climate change is mostly the result of [man-made] sources. **A similar proportion 'strongly disagree.'** Furthermore, **only 22.8% of respondents 'strongly agree' that the [UN] International Panel on Climate Change reports accurately reflect a consensus within climate science."** [Emphasis added]

NO! In an "open letter" to the Canadian Government entitled "Open Kyoto to Debate," published in the Canadian National Post in 2006, 60 scientists said: "When the public comes to understand that **there is no 'consensus' among climate scientists** about the relative importance of the various causes of global climate change, the government will be in a far better position to develop plans that reflect reality and so benefit both the environment and the economy." [Emphasis added]

NO! Dr. Bob Carter, Marine Geophysical Laboratory, James Cook University, Australia, wrote: **"[Al] Gore's circumstantial arguments are so weak that they are pathetic.** It is simply incredible that they, and his film, are commending public attention." [Emphasis added]

NO! As reported in PRNewswire-USNewswire, Washington, DC, September 12, 2007: An analysis of peer-reviewed literature revealed that **500 scientists had published evidence refuting at least one element of current man-made global warming scares.** More than 300 of the scientists found evidence that 1) a natural moderate 1,500-year climate cycle has produced previous warmings similar to the present, 2) present modern warming is linked strongly to variations in the sun's irradiance. The list of these scientists may be found in the recent Avery and Singer book, *Unstoppable Global Warming: Every 1,500 Years*, Rowman & Littlefield, 2007.

The public needs to understand that there is no consensus among climate scientists about the relative importance of the various causes of global climate change.

Is there scientific consensus that "Global Warming" is true?

NO! Medical researcher Dr. Klaus-Martin Schulte examined all research papers on climate change published between 2004 and February 2007. The results were submitted to the journal *Energy and Environment*.

NO! Of the 528 papers, only 38 (7%) strongly endorsed consensus. The total for implied endorsement was 45%.

NO! Only 32 papers (6%) strongly rejected consensus.

NO! However, 254 papers (49%) were neutral, neither accepting nor rejecting consensus.

NO! Only 1 paper (0.2%) made any reference to climate change leading to catastrophic results.

NO! THIS IS NOT CONSENSUS!

Avery and Singer note: ". . . we have compelling evidence of a real-world climate cycle averaging 1,470 years (plus or minus 500) . . . The climate cycle has above all been moderate, and the trees, bears, birds, and humans have quietly adapted."

Al Gore's movie "An Inconvenient Truth" - Is there any truth in it?

NO! The first casualty in this Environmental Terrorist movie is truth.

NO! The movie is full of half lies, lies and total misinformation.

Al Gore claimed that the drying up of Lake Chad was an example of global warming.

What is the truth?

The watersheds that feed Lake Chad—once the size of Vermont but now the size of Rhode Island—have been desiccated by drought since the mid-20th century. The reduction in the size of the Lake is a direct result of population increase, irrigation for agriculture, overgrazing and regional climate variability. In a similar way, the Aral Sea dried up because the Russian government diverted 75% of the water going

119

into it in order to irrigate agricultural lands.

<u>Al Gore claimed that the disappearance of snow on Mt. Kilimanjaro was expressly attributable to human-induced climate change.</u>

What is the truth?

Mt. Kilimanjaro is colder today than in 1970. Studies reported in the journals *Science* in 2003; *International Journal of Climatology* in 2004; and, *Journal of Geophysical Research* in 2004 concluded that the snow cap of Mt. Kilimanjaro has been shrinking since 1880, the end of "The Little Ice Age," because the forest around the mountain have been cut down, thus reducing the humidity needed to build the snow pack, and there has been a short term increase in solar heating.

<u>Al Gore claimed that Hurricane Katrina was a direct result of global warming.</u>

What is the truth?

It is impossible to link an individual hurricane to any type of weather or climate change. Single storms cannot be used to determine large scale long term changes. **(Three strikes and you are out?)**

The Environmental Terrorists are not primarily focused on the consequences of climate change. They are primarily interested in growing an industry that makes them very rich, very powerful and very famous.

Al Gore referenced the "Little Ice Age," but not the Medieval Warm Period ("Medieval Optimum") that preceded it. <u>Al Gore claimed that</u> ". . . if you look at the hottest years ever measured in this atmospheric record, they have all occurred in the last 14 years. **The hottest of all was 2005."** [Emphasis added]

What is the truth?

Actually, 1998 was the hottest year on record; however, since then ground temperatures have remained stable. In a similar way, ocean temperatures have not increased.

Dr. Bob Carter, geologist, James Cook University, Queensland, Australia, noted that: "the official temperature records of the Climate Research Unit at the University of East Anglia (UK), [show] that for the years 1998-2005 global average temperature did not increase." ["There IS a problem with global warming . . . it stopped in 1998," Daily Telegraph (UK), April 9, 2006.]

It should be noted that Al Gore used the extreme Canadian and United Kingdom predictions of temperature increases of 14.4 F and 5.4 F by the year 2100. Al Gore did not use the lower increases of 1.8 F predicted by the US National Center for Atmospheric Research and other modelers at The National Center for Policy Analysis. The NCAR model is far more sophisticated than the Canadian or UK models. **The measured rate is only 0.17 C/decade (0.306 F/decade) for the past 37 years.**

If the earth is warming because of human action; **why are the polar ice caps on Mars getting smaller, at the same time?** Might not this indicate that an increase in solar activity was responsible and that any warming on earth was not due to human action?

Al Gore claimed sea-level would rise up to 20 feet [6 meters] because of melting ice in either Western Antarctica or Greenland. A significant amount of his film was devoted to showing alarming predictions of flooding in major coastal population centers, specifically Florida, San Francisco, New York, Bangladesh, China and the Netherlands.

What is the truth?

Even the far-left United Nations International Panel on Climate Change [IPCC] has reported that: "No significant acceleration in the rate of sea-level rise during the 20th century has been detected." The UN IPCC predicts that sea-level will rise only about 38.5 cm [15 inches] by 2100.

"[a] 2005 joint statement by the science academies of the Western nations, including the U.S. NAS, actually estimates a worst-case scenario of 35 inches." [P. Stanway, "An Inconvenient Truth for Gore," Edmonton Sun, July 7, 2006]

Question: If sea-levels are rising rapidly, why is the Maldives Island government lobbying the European Union to help fund ocean front development there?

Melting sea ice does not raise sea-level (it lowers it); only ice melting off the land will raise sea-level. Ocean levels have been rising for centuries. Each year on average, 1 cubic mile (4 cubic Km) of Juvenile Water is added to the earth's surface through geothermal events [volcanoes, mineral springs]. NASA found that the net ice loss from Greenland and Antarctica would raise sea-level 0.002 inches (0.05 mm)/year between 1992 and 2002: or, 2 inches (five cm)/1,000 years. Greenland was about 1 C (1.8 F) warmer in 1925 than it is today. Yet this was only about 30 years after we came out of "The Little Ice Age."

What is the truth?

Erik the Red sailed to uninhabited Greenland in AD 982. Showing an intuitive flair for PR, Erik sent back word of a bountiful "green land" in order to entice others to follow him and colonize the southwestern tip of the island. **Those Nordic settlements survived for over 300 years** until disappearing at the beginning of the Little Ice Age.

An international team of scientists has drilled 1.2 miles [2 Km] deep into the Greenland ice sheet (underneath the bottom of the ice cap) and found: "that the area [had once been] populated by diverse forests made up of alders, spruce, pine, and members of the yew family. Living in the trees and on the forest floor was a wide variety of insect life, including beetles, flies, spiders, butterflies and moths." They found DNA of spiders and trees. This indicates that Greenland's ice is less susceptible to meltdown than had been predicted by computer models of climate change. **"This may have implications for how the ice sheets respond to global warming. They may withstand rising temperatures."** [Emphasis added] [Willerslev, Eske, evolutionary biologist, University of Copenhagen, *Science*, July 6, 2007, vol. 317, p. 11]

Environmental Terrorists claim that the Polar Bears are dying from "global warming." The truth is that Polar Bear populations are growing where it is getting warmer, and getting smaller where it is getting colder. [Dr. Mitchell Taylor, Canadian Polar Bear Biologist, Depart. of the Environment, Gov. of Nunavut]

Grey Whale populations are also increasing in the warmer Arctic waters. [J. Kay, San Francisco Chronicle newspaper, June 28, 2006]

Dr. Ian Stirling of the Canadian Wildlife Service said: "Swimming 100 miles is not a big deal for a polar bear, <u>especially a fat one</u>." [Emphasis added]

Al Gore claimed in his movie that Polar Bears were dying as a direct result of global warming.

What is the truth?

The four dead polar bears shown in the movie **died when they were unexpectedly caught in a severe storm.**

Al Gore claimed in his movie that some Pacific atolls had to be evacuated because of rising sea water levels.

What is the truth?

Pacific atolls have not been evacuated because of "rising" sea levels.

At a Senate hearing on Capitol Hill, Syun-Ichi Akasofu said that highly publicized climate models showing a disappearing Arctic were nothing more than "science fiction." [Syun-Ichi Akasofu, Director of the International Arctic Research Center, Fairbanks, AK, April 2007]

The Antarctic ice cap is not melting away. At this time, it is growing in its total amount of ice; only the surface area is changing.

"The net ice balance in Antarctica is positive; it is gaining ice." Antarctica "will contribute to reduction in sea level because it is gaining ice . . . The net **ice balance in Greenland is very close to neutral.** . . . <u>There have been three periods in the last 2,000 years in which Alaska was as warm as it is now</u>." [Dr. Michaels, Climatologist] [Emphasis added]

The oceans have been cooling on average for the past 4,500 years; since the end of Noah's Flood.

Al Gore claimed in his movie that glaciers around the world were all receding because of global warming. The Upsala Glacier in Patagonia <u>is retreating</u>; however, **30 miles (50 km) away,** the Perito Moreno Glacier <u>is advancing</u>. In fact, nearby medium-sized glaciers are stable and large-sized glaciers **are advancing rapidly. Pio XI, the largest glacier in South America is advancing very quickly.**

123

The reason that glaciers are melting in some parts of the Andes: "climatic change in the Venezuelan Andes is linked to changes in solar activity during the Little Ice Age" and "... **solar variability is the primary underlying cause of the glacier fluctuations"** (Dr. P. J. Polissar, "Solar Modulation of Little Ice Age Climate in the Tropical Andes," June 1, 2006, *Proceedings of the National Academy of Sciences USA* [emphasis added]).

Hint: It is variations in the Sun's temperature, not Man-made global warming, that is causing fluctuations in the glaciers!

"Glaciers are advancing in the European Arctic. These are episodic events. The Arctic does occasionally get warmer and colder. Climate change is the norm. **If you want something to worry about, it would be if the climate were static.** It would be like a person being dead" (Dr. Richard Lindzen, Alfred P. Sloan Professor of Meteorology at MIT, former lead author, UN IPCC[emphasis added]).

For every glacier in the world that is receding, there is one that is advancing.

Concerning consensus on "global warming": Al Gore stated, "A survey of more than 928 scientific papers in respected journals shows 100% agreement."

First, if there were "more than 928," **just how many were there?**

Second, the 928 papers Gore mentioned **were not unanimous on the issue at hand.**

Third, the 928 papers were carefully hand selected and **represented less than 10% of the over 11,000 relevant papers** published during that time frame (1993–2006).

Al Gore claimed in his movie that carbon dioxide is a greenhouse gas that causes "Global Warming." **Actually,** temperature rise comes first, and then this causes carbon dioxide increases as more plants grow, and warmer oceans release more carbon dioxide than colder oceans.

Al Gore claimed that hurricanes were continuously getting stronger and more frequent because of global warming. The National Oceanic and Atmospheric Administration (NOAA) has found no statistical increase in hurricanes, only the normal 40 to 50 year hurricane cycle.

The increase in damages to man-made structures is due to humans continuing to build more and more buildings along coastlines and on known flood plains. The US National Hurricane Center found that 1941-1950 was the most active hurricane decade on record. Two-thirds of the largest hurricanes to hit the US between 1851 and 2004 occurred prior to 1950. **Between 1961 and 2000 the number and intensity of hurricanes hitting the US fell significantly.**

God uses weather to judge those who are His (Amos 4:7).

In 2005, the *Bulletin of the American Meteorological Society* made three points:

1) There is no established connection between greenhouse gases and the number of hurricanes.

2) Any future changes in hurricanes will be small and within normal variations.

3) The politics of linking hurricanes to global warming threatens to undermine support for legitimate climate research.

The Twentieth Century is neither unprecedented in its warmth nor historically aberrant (*Bulletin of the American Meteorological Society*, November 2005, pp. 1571–75).

Al Gore claimed in his movie that global warming was going to stop the Gulf Stream from flowing.

What is the truth?

In order for the Gulf Stream to stop flowing, the earth would have to stop rotating! Such claims are extreme hyperbole used to promote the irrational belief system of Environmental Terrorists, like Mr. Gore.

Al Gore claimed in his movie that drought was increasing worldwide and that deserts were getting bigger because of global warming. But, since the mid-1980s, **the Sahara Desert has been receding** along its southern border as more rain has fallen because of "global warming."

Al Gore claimed in his movie that "The debate is over . . . The scientific consensus has settled the issue of global warming." This is obviously a false claim; there is no such consensus among scientists. The debate is contentious and going strong.

In his movie, Al Gore gave lengthy tribute to his Harvard science professor, Dr. Roger Revelle, for enchanting him with the concepts of carbon dioxide emissions causing global warming. However, **Dr. Revelle has utterly rejected Al Gore's global warming extremism.**

Al Gore claims to be pro-science. However, as Vice President of the US he fired any scientist in the federal government who dared to question even the most extremist pro-greenhouse doomsayers (*National Review* editorial, June 1994).

Al Gore smears anyone who disagrees with him by calling them "pseudo-scientists," accusing them of being bought off by the energy industry. **Nothing could be further from the truth!** Many competent scientists, many of them evolutionists, disagree with Gore about "global warming." Even Patrick Moore, the cofounder of the radically left environmental group Greenpeace, now says that **we should be considering going back to clean nuclear energy.** It was the Clinton-Gore administration that, without Congressional approval, declared America's largest deposit of clean, low-sulfur coal in southern Utah to be part of a national monument and off-limits to mining.

Dr. Don J. Easterbrook (a global warming proponent), Professor Emeritus of Geology, Western Washington University, gave remarks about Gore's film to the annual meeting of the Geological Society of America in 2007. He said that Gore's film has: "… a lot of inaccuracies in the statements we are seeing, and we have to temper that with real data."

Gore claimed that: "our civilization has never experienced any environmental shift similar to this" threatened change. Dr. Easterbrook showed a slide of temperature trends for the supposed past 15,000 years. It highlighted 10 major swings, including the Medieval Warm Period. He noted that these swings were up to "20 times greater than the warming in the past century."

Dr. Richard S. Lindzen is the Alfred P. Sloan Professor of Atmospheric Sciences at MIT; a member of the National Academy of Sciences USA; and former lead author, UN IPCC (International Panel on Climate Change). In the *Wall Street Journal*, **Dr. Richard Lindzen accused**

Gore of "shrill alarmism."

Al Gore claimed in his movie that global warming was causing the spreading of infectious diseases, such as malaria, around the world. He implied that because of this, **we were all going to die.**

Dr. Paul Reiter is the Director of the Insects and Infectious Diseases Unit of the Pasteur Institute in Paris. In the *International Herald Tribune*, January, 2007, **Dr. Reiter faulted Gore's portrayal of global warming as responsible for spreading malaria.** "For 12 years, my colleagues and I have protested against the[se] unsubstantiated claims. We have done the studies and **challenged the alarmists, but they continue to ignore the facts**" (emphasis added).

Dr. Richard S. Lindzen made this prophetic statement:

> **Future generations will wonder in bemused amazement that the early twenty-first century's developed world went into hysterical panic over a globally averaged temperature increase of a few tenths of a degree, and, on the basis of gross exaggerations of highly uncertain computer projections combined into implausible chains of inference, proceeded to contemplate a rollback of the industrial age** (emphasis added).

Al Gore claimed in his movie that **temperatures were at their highest level in 1,000 years.** The National Academy of Sciences USA reported that the current highs appeared unrivaled since only 1600, the tail end of a temperature rise known as the Medieval Warm Period (*NAS Report*, June 2006).

Dr. Benny J. Peiser is a Social Anthropologist with the Cambridge-Conference Network. He noted that: **"Hardly a week goes by without a new research paper that questions part or even some basics of climate change theory"** (emphasis added). Some reports offer alternatives to human activity as the source of global warming.

Dr. Robert M. Carter is a Marine Geologist at James Cook University in Australia. He wrote: **"Nowhere does Mr. Gore tell his audience that all of the phenomena that he describes fall within the natural range of environmental change on our planet. Nor does he present** any evidence that climate during the 20th century departed discernibly from its historical pattern of constant change" (emphasis added).

Dr. James E. Hansen is the Director of NASA's Goddard Institute for Space Studies, and an advisor to Al Gore on environmental issues. He is the recipient of a $720,000 grant from George Soros. Commenting about Gore's film, a film on which he was a paid advisor, Dr. Hansen wrote that the film may have "imperfections" and "technical flaws."

Environmental Terrorists: What Are Their Motivations?

1) The politicians and bureaucrats sell the issue as an "emergency" to justify huge increases in taxes, government power and government regulation.

2) Most atmospheric scientists work for government and their income and grants are dependent upon increasing the size of government.

3) The Hollywood liberals use "global warming" to plug their latest movies.

4) Environmental terrorists need crises to promote their huge fund-raising efforts.

What Are The Top Ten Myths of Environmentalism?

1. It is HOT in here!

This myth is promoted by any environmental terrorist groups, including the National Geographic Society. Consider what they said in 2006:

> **The planet is heating up—and fast.** Glaciers are melting, sea levels are rising, cloud forests are drying, and wildlife is scrambling to keep pace. **It's becoming clear that humans have caused most of the past century's warming** by releasing heat-trapping gases as we power our modern lives. Called greenhouse gases, their levels are higher now than in the last 650,000 years. . . . What will

128

we do to slow this warming? How will we cope with the changes we've already set into motion? While we struggle to figure it all out, **the face of the Earth as we know it . . . hangs in the balance"** ("What Is Global Warming?" *National Geographic,* [On-Line] 2006 [emphasis added]).

It is HOT in here! Compared to when? It is cooler now than it was at the end of the 1930s or during the Medieval Warm Period. It was hotter in 1939 than it is today.

2. The 1990s were the hottest decade on record. <u>The National Academy of Sciences USA debunked this myth in 2006</u>. It was warmer in the US in 1936 than it was in 2002. The 1990s were not the hottest decade on record.

3. "The science is settled"; carbon dioxide causes global warming. This is a myth and a travesty of "science." Historically, **carbon dioxide gas in the atmosphere increases only after global warming,** <u>not before it</u>.

A USC study concluded that deep-sea temperatures rose 1,300 years before the rise in atmospheric carbon dioxide, which would rule out this supposed "greenhouse gas" as the main agent of the meltdown. "There has been this continual reference to the correspondence between carbon dioxide and climate change as reflected in ice core records as justification for the role of carbon dioxide in climate change. **You can no longer argue that carbon dioxide alone caused the end of the ice ages"** (Stott, Lowell USC geologist, peer-reviewed study in *Science,* November 2007 [emphasis added]).

There was only a very slight rise in the parts per million concentration of carbon dioxide gas in the earth's atmosphere from 1920 to 1960 (from 300 ppm to 320 ppm), hardly anything to be alarmed about. **If this is all so "settled" science,** as environmental terrorists claim, **why are we spending $5 billion more each year to research it?** Attempting to stifle debate is inherently anti-scientific.

4. The climate was stable until Man came along. This is a totally mythological statement. The "poster child" of this myth is a supposed graph of the average temperatures on earth for the past 1,000 years, and presented in the shape of a "hockey stick" lying on its side. **It is**

a disgrace and has even been thrown out by the United Nation's IPCC. The "hockey stick" graph is a total fabrication, an intentionally deceptive invention that erased the entire Medieval Warm Period. **This is not just bad science, it is criminal intent.**

5. The glaciers are melting. This is a myth that goes both ways. Glaciers are receding; and, glaciers are advancing all over the earth, even in the same areas that other glaciers are receding. **Global warming and global cooling cannot both be true at the same time.** Data from the World Glacier Monitoring Service indicates that the number of receding and advancing glaciers is roughly equal.

6. Climate change is raising the sea levels. Even the UN IPCC found no statistically significant change in the rate of increase of sea level over the past century. Australia and New Zealand report no increase in sea level, and may even be seeing a sea level drop. The latest research suggests that sea levels would decline, not rise, if temperatures rise, due to increased evaporation from the oceans and subsequent precipitation on to the land.

7. Climate change is the greatest threat to the world's poor. This is an insidious myth that is without basis. Climate and weather patterns have always changed, and they always will! Advanced societies adapt best with superior infrastructures and non-rationed access to energy. Poor societies suffer because of the lack of infrastructure and the rationing of access to energy.

8. "Global warming" means more frequent, more severe storms. This is a myth that the UN IPCC no longer supports. Storms are cyclical and are not more frequent or more severe than in the past. Based upon grouping hurricanes that have hit the US into fifty year segments, the number and severity of hurricanes has gone down since 1950.

9. "Global warming" proposals are about the environment. This myth is only true if it means that **"global warming" proposals will make the environment worse!** Actually, "wealthier is healthier, and cleaner." The Kyoto Protocol has a negative effect on any nation that signs it. Even the European Union Environmental Commissioner admitted that Kyoto is "about competition, about leveling the playing field for big business worldwide." **It penalizes the successful and promotes those who pollute the environment most!**

10. The U.S. is going it alone on Kyoto and "global warming." THIS MYTH IS PURE NONSENSE! The U.S. and 155 other nations rejected the Kyoto Protocol's energy rationing scheme. These 156 countries represent most of the world's population, most of the world's economic activity, and most of the world's areas of projected future economic growth. The Kyoto Protocol was signed by European nations, and about one dozen others (none of whom are in fact presently reducing their pollution emissions).

These ten myths, like any good story, are useful only to those who proffer them, but they have little grounding in facts. "Global warming" is not catastrophic, not man-made, nor global.

Is the 1997 Kyoto Protocol good or bad for the world?

The Kyoto Protocol treaty required that the G-8 nations had to reduce "greenhouse gas" emissions, **but the treaty exempted: Communist China, India, Brazil and other large "developing nations."** "Greenhouse gas" emissions from Communist China and India will exceed those of the US within ten years. Communist China will construct over 500 new coal-burning power plants in the next ten years; that is, one a week. **The purchase of "pollution credits," or "carbon credits" is merely giving someone money for nothing in return.** Historically, this scheme may go down in history as the greatest con job ever devised. In 2000, then President of France, Jacques Chirac, called Kyoto "the first component of authentic global governance [a one world government]."

Please ponder these points:

1. Al Gore signed the treaty on behalf of the USA, **but the US Senate refused to ratify.**

2. In the 1990s, the US Department of Energy estimated that implementing the Kyoto Protocol in the US would:

a) Increase gasoline costs by 14 to 66 cents per gallon

b) Increase electric bills by an average of 86%

c) Increase coal prices by 153%

d) Decrease GNP growth to 1.9% instead of increase it to 3.5%

e) Increase costs by $77 to $338 billion per year

3. The Kyoto Protocol drives up prices, increases government control, limits use of energy, but will not prevent one-tenth of one degree warming over the next 50 years.

4. In May 2007, Canada dropped out of the Kyoto Protocol because of its adverse effect on the Canadian economy.

5. Russia signed the Kyoto Protocol only after being granted (bribed with) huge "pollution credits" that Russia could then sell back to the European countries for hard currency.

6. The highly respected climatologist, Dr. Richard S. Lindzen of Harvard, told President George W. Bush that even if alarmist predictions were to come true, "Kyoto would be to do nothing at great expense."

7. Even the environmentalist Peter Roderick, Friends of the Earth International, said "I think everybody agrees that Kyoto is really, really hopeless in terms of delivering what the planet needs."

What Are the Problems in Measuring Global Warming or Cooling?

The most powerful tools science has developed to predict climate and weather changes are computer models. **Computer models are recognized as consistently and inherently flawed** because of the bias of the computer programmer to get the desired results. How can environmental terrorists predict climate and weather conditions 20, 50 or 100 years from now, **when these models cannot predict if it will rain next Thursday?** More than 30 major computer climate models exist; no two agree on the results.

In the 1990s, "global warming" coincided with the closing of thousands of temperature reporting stations, mostly in the colder parts of

Russia. If you leave out temperatures from the colder parts of the world, the average will obviously go up. (From 1989 through 2000, about two-thirds [10,000 of 15,000] of the world's temperature recording stations were closed, mostly in the former USSR. At the same time, the average global temperature, for the decade of 1990–2000, went up about two-thirds of a degree C.) Weather stations in poorer countries are maintained differently than in wealthier countries. The "global mean surface temperature" means about as much as the "global mean telephone number."

Global warming, if it were true, might produce the effect of global cooling. Global warming would produce more evaporation leading to increases in rain, snow and perhaps trigger a sudden new ice age.

What Is the Historically Correct Perspective?

The earth was significantly warmer thousands of years ago. Many dinosaur fossils have been found near the South Pole. Dinosaur bones and tracks have been found on Svalbard (north of Norway); on the North Slope of Alaska; in northern Canada from the Yukon Territory to the Queen Elizabeth Islands; and in central Siberia. In 1999, Duck-billed dinosaur bones were found on the North Slope of Alaska. A duck-bill dinosaur tooth was recently found on James Ross Island. Eight types of dinosaurs have now been found on the North Slope in Alaska. All eight have also been found at lower latitudes. In 1883, fossil Breadfruit leaves and fruit were found in western Greenland. Breadfruit only grows between temperatures of 59 to 101 F (+15 to +38 C).

The Medieval Warm Period was produced by a "solar maximum" that occurs in roughly 1,000-1,500 year cycles. From 1250 AD to 1900 AD we had the "Little Ice Age," Frost Fairs on the frozen River Thames, and in 1816 "The Year Without Summer." Another solar warm cycle began around 1850 and we are at the end of it now, with a cooling trend to be expected soon.

In 2004, cores of the Alpha Ridge (bottom of the Arctic Ocean) proved that in the past the water temperature had been 59 to 68 F (+15 to +20 C).

At this time, the Southern Hemisphere is cooling and the Northern

Hemisphere is warming slightly. **At this time,** the Antarctic is getting measurably colder! At the South Pole temperatures have fallen since 1957. During the American Dust Bowl, people were talking about global warming, but the temperatures were dropping.

In 1895, the New York Times newspaper warned of a coming new ice age. Subsequently, it ran these headlines:

The sinking of the RMS Titanic had a supposed link to a coming new ice age. On October 7, 1912, the New York Times headline was: **"Prof. Schmidt Warns us of an Encroaching Ice Age"**

Sept. 18, 1924: **"MacMillan Reports Signs of New Ice Age"**

March 27, 1933: **"America in Longest Warming Spell Since 1776; Temperature Line Records a 25-Year Rise"**

May 21, 1975: **"Scientists Ponder Why World's Climate Is Changing; A Major Cooling Widely Considered to Be Inevitable"**

Dec. 27, 2005: **"Past Hot Times Hold Few Reasons to Relax About New Warming"**

Wait a minute. If in 1895 and 1924 we had signs of a coming ice age, how in 1933 could we have the longest warming period since 1776; and, how could temperatures have been rising for 25 straight years (since 1908)? The first answer is simple. We had just come out of the Little Ice Age. The second answer is that this was the political agenda of Environmental Terrorists 90 years ago.

On April 11, 2007, Dr. Plimer (Geology Professor at Adelaide U.) spoke to the Australian Institute of Mining and Metallurgy: **"When meteorologists can change the weather then we can start to think about humans changing climate"** (emphasis added).

In 1801, British astronomer William Herschel reported that when sunspots were numerous, grain prices fell; when sunspots were few, grain prices rose.

In 2001, a study of cloud cover over the USA from 1900 to 1987 was published. The founding was that average cloud cover increased and decreased in lock step with the sun's 11-year sunspot cycle. The most plausible cause: changes in the UV light the sun delivers to the

134

stratosphere. The amount of cosmic rays that reach deep into the atmosphere changes the amount of cloud cover. The valve controlling the flow of cosmic rays from deep in space is the sun's magnetic field. The sun's magnetic field fluctuates in direct proportion to the fluctuating strength of solar sunspot activity.

Clouds can cool the earth, or clouds can heat the earth. Depending on how thick and how high or low they are in altitude: low clouds cool the planet by reflecting sunlight back into outer space; high clouds act as a blanket and trap heat in the atmosphere. Peak periods of sunspot activity deliver more sunlight to the top of the atmosphere than minimum periods of sunspot activity. During swings in sunspot cycles, the largest change is in UV light. Much of this UV light is absorbed by ozone in the stratosphere (6 to 30 miles up). The rise and fall of UV light alters the amount of heat-trapping ozone. Instead of warming the troposphere (0 to 6 miles up), changes in solar UV output redistribute heat, cold, rain, etc. Clearly, it is the sun that is driving weather and climate fluctuations.

1970 - Birth of the Modern Environmental Terrorist Movement

The first Earth Day was April 22, 1970.

The EPA was formed in July, 1970.

The Clean Air Act was enacted in 1970.

The Clean Water Act was enacted in 1972.

The Endangered Species Act was enacted in 1973.

The environmental extremists of the 1960s and 1970s now hold powerful political positions and their ideas permeate public policy.

Since 1970, a flood of environmental propaganda and eco-myths have followed:

Hairspray is depleting the Ozone!

The internal (infernal) combustion engine is evil!

Technology contaminates the environment!

Capitalism is evil, evil, evil!

To environmental terrorists humans are <u>unnatural and a cancer on the land!</u> To the true blue environmental terrorist the issue is their irrational religion. **Friends of the Earth International (2007): "[T]he Earth is a creation to be honored and respected as our Mother."** The environmental terrorist group, Optimum Population Trust, insists that children are the greatest threat to the planet; that parents should have one less child in order to stop global warming and save the planet (*The Australian*, March 7, 2007). Their religion drives them into a form of insanity. For example: Researchers in Norway claim that their national animal, the moose, is harming the climate by emitting over 2,000 kilos (over two tons) of carbon dioxide per year (*Spiegel*, August 21, 2007). But Australian scientists are very happy because kangaroos produce almost no methane (*Fox News*, December 6, 2007).

In the 1970's these Environmental Terrorists, and their ilk, told us boldly that we were about to enter the "Twilight Zone of Humanity" because **we were heading irrevocably into the next "Ice Age."**

The <u>1974</u> Global Cooling Disaster Remembered

In 1974, *Time* magazine warned its readers that the world may be on the verge of a catastrophic climate disaster: **Global Cooling!** *Time* reported a three decade-long cooling and other "weather aberrations."

In 1974, in *Time* magazine, a University of Toronto climatologist [referring to global cooling] said: **"I don't believe that the world's present population is sustainable if there are more than three years like 1972 in a row"** (emphasis added).

On July 24, 1974, *Time* magazine published an article entitled: "Another Ice Age?" The first paragraph included:

"... However widely the weather varies ... when meteorologists take an average of temperatures around the globe **they find that the atmosphere has been growing gradually cooler for the past three decades. The trend shows no indication of reversing. Climatological Cassandra's are becoming increasingly apprehensive, for the weather aberrations they are studying may be the harbinger of another ice age"** (emphasis added).

136

The last paragraph of the article stated:

"Whatever the cause of **the cooling trend, its effects could be extremely serious, if not catastrophic.** Scientists figure that only a 1% decrease in the amount of sunlight hitting the earth's surface could tip the climate balance, **and cool the planet enough to send it sliding down the road to another ice age within only a few hundred years"** (emphasis added).

The <u>1975</u> Global Cooling Disaster Remembered

In *Science Digest*, 1975, Douglas Colligan wrote: "[T]he world's climatologists are agreed. . . . **Once the freeze starts, it will be too late."** (emphasis added).

On April 28, 1975, *Newsweek* magazine printed an article entitled "The Cooling World" in which it quoted the National Academy of Sciences, USA:

"A major climatic change would force economic and social adjustments on a worldwide scale."

"There are ominous signs that the Earth's weather patterns have begun to change dramatically and that these changes may portend a drastic decline in food production . . . The drop in food production could begin quite soon. . . . The evidence in support of these predictions has now begun to accumulate so massively that meteorologists are hard-pressed to keep up with it" (emphasis added).

In 2006, US Senator James Inhofe, Chairman of the Senate Committee on Environment and Public Works, commented on Fox News that the current global warming climate scare had no more basis in reality than the last climate scare (Global Cooling 1954-1980). "This whole concept of another Ice Age is probably the greatest single hoax ever perpetuated on the American people . . . **And it was until this thing** [meaning the current scare over "global warming"] **came along"** (emphasis added).

The <u>1976</u> Global Cooling Disaster Remembered

In 1976, *Newsweek* warned that because of global cooling, ". . . this trend will reduce agricultural productivity for the rest of the century."

Back in 1954, *Fortune* had published an article saying: "Despite all you may have read, heard, or imagined, **it's been growing cooler— not warmer—since the Thirties"** (emphasis added).

In 1976, Lowell Ponte wrote in *The Cooling*:

> It is a cold fact: the Global Cooling presents humankind with the most important social, political, and adaptive challenge we have had to deal with . . . Your stake in the decisions we make concerning it is of ultimate importance; the survival of ourselves, our children, our species."

While using poor science and gross overstatements, he gives us the essence of the concern that Environmental Terrorists had about "Global Cooling" in 1976.

The <u>2006</u> Global Cooling Disaster Predicted?

In November 2006, the Russian Academy of Science warned about the ice age returning.

What Is the Historically Correct Perspective?

What causes climate changes? The September 2006 *New Scientist* said that it was the "prolonged lulls in **the sun's activity**–the sunspots and dramatic flares that are driven by its powerful magnetic field" (emphasis added).

The "sun still appears to be the main forcing agent in global climate change" (Svensmark, H. and E. Friis-Christiensen, *The Persistent Role of the Sun in Climate Forcing*, Danish National Space Center Scientific Report, March 2007 [emphasis added]).

With apologies to the Democratic Party pundit, James Carville: **"It's the sun, stupid."**

138

What Are the Facts about Recent Global Temperatures?

NOAA has accurate US temperature measurements from 1895 to 2008. Things got warmer from 1895 to the 1940s. The steepest trend was from 1910 to 1935. This was before significant use of fossil fuels. The US cooled for the next three and a half decades, sparking the "global cooling" panic that ended in the late-1970s. The rate of warming from 1910 to 1934 (a period of limited fossil fuel use) is steeper than the rate of warming from 1975 to 1998 (a period of significant fossil fuel consumption).

1934 and 1998 were the two hottest years on record: 1934 was the height of the Dust Bowl and 1998 was an extreme El Nino spike. From 1975 to 1998, the country warmed. During that time, fossil fuel consumption went up and solar heating increased because of an increase in solar activity. There has been a slight cooling trend since 1998 despite fossil fuel consumption increases in China and India. In 2007, the U.S. absorbed more CO_2 than it emitted, while the EU countries emission of CO_2 has gone up steadily since the Kyoto Protocol was signed.

In summary, according to environmental terrorists:

From 1895-1930: We Experienced Catastrophic <u>Natural</u> Global Cooling

From 1930-1954: We Experienced Catastrophic <u>Natural</u> Global Warming

From 1954-1980: We Experienced Catastrophic *Man-made* Global Cooling

From 1980-2008: We Experienced Catastrophic *Man-made* Global Warming

NOTE: They change their opinion in 25 to 35 year cycles!

Man is not in charge of the climate and the weather. **God is in charge of the weather! (Matt. 5:45)**

What Are Some the Potential Benefits If Global Warming Were True?

1) **The fabled Northwest Passage** between the Atlantic and Pacific **would become a reality** cutting shipping time in half. In August, 2005, the Russian ship *Akademik Fyodorov*, became the first ship to cross the North Pole without the use of an icebreaker.

2) If Arctic ice melted significantly, **25% of the earth's oil and natural gas reserves would become available for extraction.**

3) Less Arctic ice would **open new fishing grounds and tourist destinations.** In 2001, Russia applied to the UN to annex one half of the Arctic Ocean, including the North Pole, as a part of Russian territory based on the new ability to map the ocean floor. In 2007, two Russian research submarines attempted to plant flags on the Arctic Ocean floor in a bid to further the Russian claim to the North Pole as a part of their sovereign territory.

4) **Melting icebergs calved from glaciers release nutrients** yielding a fivefold increase in phytoplankton and higher predators out to a distance of 2.3 miles (*Science News*, July 7, 2007, Vol. 172, p. 13).

5) **Perhaps the Vikings could reestablish their settlements in Greenland** that they had to abandon 700 years ago at the beginning of the "Little Ice Age."

6) **Cold kills while heat kills less often.** According to the UK Department of Health, if the southern UK warmed by 3 C by 2050, then 2,000 more would die from summer heat waves while 20,000 fewer would die from cold in the winter.

7) If the temperature in Canada were to rise only about 3 F, **the wheat growing area would reach as far north as Hudson Bay,** and grapevines could be cultivated in southern Canada.

8) If the Earth were warming, **more water would be evaporating, producing more rain for food crops and timber production;** and,

producing more snow that would rebuild the polar ice caps; and, more glaciers would be advancing.

9) If the Earth were warming, **there would be longer growing seasons and warmer winter nights.**

Every global warming period of the past has produced a net increase in economic and social benefits! "Two thousand years of published human histories say that the warm periods were good for people. It was the harsh, unstable Dark Ages and Little Ice Age that brought bigger storms, untimely frost, widespread famine and plagues of disease" (Avery, Dennis and S. Fred Singer, *Unstoppable Global Warming: Every 1,500 Years* [emphasis added]).

What Actually Causes Global Warming?

1) **Natural processes** such as sunlight, heat released by volcanoes and the heat released by radioactive decay in the earth's crust.

2) The four **solar cycles;** combined with the increase and decrease in sun spots and the increase and decrease in the sun's magnetic field.

"Humans have long known since the invention of the telescope that **the earth's climate variations were linked to the sunspot cycle,** but we had not understood how. Recent experiments have demonstrated that more or fewer cosmic rays hitting the earth create more or fewer of the low, cooling clouds that deflect solar heat back into space - amplifying small variations in the intensity of the sun" (Avery, Dennis and S. Fred Singer, *Unstoppable Global Warming: Every 1,500 Years* [emphasis added]).

3) The **Earth's wobble and eccentric orbit** exposes the surface to varying amounts of heat at different periods of time.

4) Snow and ice reflect heat, but **water absorbs it.**

5) **A clear sky** allows solar heating of surfaces.

6) **Land use changes,** natural or Man-made.

141

7) The older the Sun gets, **the hotter it burns!**

8) **Surface temperatures rise** in city areas as more asphalt and cement are poured in those areas (atmospheric temperatures are not increasing!).

9) **"Greenhouse Gases,"** such as naturally occurring water vapor (70%), CO2 (26%), methane (9%), ozone (7%) and nitrous oxide have a warming effect. **CO2 is NOT a major "Greenhouse Gas."** It is a natural by-product of human beings and animals. It is released by plants upon death! Nitrous oxide is produced by microbes in the soil. Methane is produced in swamps, bogs, rice paddies, cows and human beings.

"Greenhouse gases" <u>are necessary for life to exist on earth</u>; **without them we would freeze to death!** Man-made combustion of fuels causes only 2% of the greenhouse gases that keep our atmosphere habitable—the other 98% are produced by purely natural causes!

<u>**THE WORLD NEEDS MORE CO2!**</u>

"'There will be significant cooling very soon,' asserted solar scientist David Archibald at the 'Greener Skies 2008' conference designed to persuade the airline industry to cut back on production of greenhouse gases to fight global warming. **Archibald asserted climate change is mostly dictated by solar cycles, not CO2 levels, and he warned they should figure ways of increasing CO2 output.** 'In a few short years, we will have a reversal of the warming of the 20th century. There will be significant cooling very soon. Our generation has known a warm, giving sun, but the new generation will suffer a sun that is less giving, and the earth will be less fruitful . . . <u>**CO2 is not even a little bit bad it's wholly beneficial**</u>'" (World Net Daily April 03, 2008 [emphasis added]).

What Actually Causes "Global Cooling"?

1) **Volcanic eruptions:** In 1991–1992 Mt. Pinatubo, in the Philippines, cooled the earth 1.26 F (0.7 C) in only one year. The eruption dumped between 20 and 30 million tons of sulphur dioxide (SO2) and other

aerosols into the atmosphere. These gases encircled the earth between the tropics in only three months, blocking out and reflecting heat and light back into outer space. In addition, there was a loss of 15% of the Ozone Layer to record lows in 1992–1993.

2) **Dust Storms:** During the American Dust Bowl (1930 to 1938), the dust blocked out 15% of sunlight and dropped the temperature 1.8 F (1 C). The American Dust Bowl was caused by an extended El Nino.

3) **The Variations of the Earth's Orbit:** The earth's orbit isn't a perfect circle; therefore the earth is slightly closer or further from the sun at different times.

4) **Smoke from Forest Fires:** Whether started by natural causes (lightening strikes) or the activity of human beings, large quantities of particulates and aerosols are injected into the atmosphere by forest fires.

5) **The Earth is Cooling Down:** The earth is radiating more heat into outer space every day than it receives from the sun. The center core temperature of the earth is 13,000 F (7,200 C). The earth has consistently lost heat since it was created.

6) **Variations in Solar Activity:** The sun is not a totally uniform heat source. The sun undergoes periodic increases and decreases in sunspot activity and magnetic field activity! These variations have a direct, significant and demonstrable effect on weather and climate changes on earth.

Nature Is Not Pristine! Volcanic eruptions are perhaps the worst "offenders." Here is a quick review of some of the record holders:

1) **The eruption of the volcano Laki, in Iceland, in 1783** is considered to be Britain's forgotten disaster. The event was catastrophic. The volcano spewed out such a large amount of sulphur dioxide and sulfuric acid that Britain was enveloped in thick smog and the sun was described as "covered like it was soaked in blood." The naturalist Gilbert White said it was "unlike anything known within the memory of man." The poet William Cowper lamented in the summer of 1783 that, "such multitudes are indisposed by fevers in this country

that farmers have difficulty gathering their harvest, the labourers having been almost every day carried out of the field incapable of work and many die." The eruption lasted for weeks and covered much of Western Europe. About one third of the population of Iceland died. Recent research by Dr. John Grattan of Aberystwyth University, Wales, has established that it was the greatest natural disaster in modern British history.

2) **The eruption of the Indonesian volcano Tambora in 1815** killed 92,000 people, hundreds of thousands of animals, spewed ash up to 800 miles away, and **produced "The Year Without Summer" in 1816.**

3) **The eruption of the Indonesian volcano Krakatau (Krakatoa), in 1883,** produced "The Sound Heard 'Round the World." The sound of the eruption was heard in downtown London, England. The eruption killed 36,000 people.

Nature Is Not Pristine! High winds are powerful, destructive and polluting. On November 13, 1970, a hurricane hit Bangladesh, killing between 500,000 and one million people. On March 18, 1925, a tornado touched down from southeastern Missouri, passing through southern Illinois and lifting up in southwestern Indiana staying on the ground for 219 miles. The result was that 625 people died, 2,000 more were injured and there was $1.7 billion in property damages (in 2007 dollars).

Nature Is Not Pristine! Floods are powerful, destructive and polluting. In 1887, the Huang He (Yellow River) in China flooded killing between 900,000 and two million people. In 1931, the Huang He flooded killing between 1 and 3.7 million people died.

Nature Is Not Pristine! Earthquakes are powerful, destructive and polluting. In 1556, the earthquake in Shensi, China, killed 830,000 people.

On Boxing Day, December 26, 2004, an earthquake measuring between 9.1 and 9.3 occurred off the coast of Southwestern Indonesia killing over 230,000 people in 11 countries. **The earthquake released 9.56 trillion tons of TNT energy (equivalent to 550 million times that of the atomic bomb dropped on Hiroshima),** or about 370 years of energy use in the United States at 2005 levels. Between 3,300 ft. and 16,500 ft. under water, it lifted a section of land 600 miles long upward 13 to 16 feet and sliding it 33 feet sideways.

Therefore, the question must be asked: "If volcanoes, winds, floods and earthquakes can accomplish so much in so little time, **why is supposed human activity receiving the full blame for supposed and unproven global warming?**"

One volcanic eruption may release more toxic gases in a given year than all human activity in that same year. Perhaps the blame is placed on human beings because **you cannot tax nor legislate against a volcano or an earthquake.** Could it be that the promotion of left-wing politics is the real reason that the truth is being withheld from the general population?

Global Warming? New Data Shows Ice Is Back!

"The Northern Hemisphere has endured its coldest winter in decades. The snow cover is the greatest since 1966. . . . the one exception—Western Europe, which had, until the weekend of Feb. 16–17 when temperatures plunged to as low as -10 C in some places, been basking in unseasonably warm weather. Around the world, vast areas have been buried under some of the heaviest snowfalls in decades. Central and Southern China, the US and Canada were hit hard by snowstorms. In China, snowfall was so heavy that over 100,000 houses collapsed under the weight of the snow." "Jerusalem, Damascus, Amman and northern Saudi Arabia reported the heaviest snow falls in years and below-zero temperatures. Baghdad had a snowstorm, the first in the memory of most residents"(Feb. 18, 2008 *London Daily Express*).

At the same time; the Athens News reported that a raging snow storm blanketed most of Greece, plunging the country into subzero freezing temperatures. The agency reported that public transport buses were at a standstill in the wider Athens area, ships remained in ports, public services remained closed, and schools and courthouses were closed.

Are the world's ice caps melting because of climate change, or are the reports just "scare mongering" by the advocates of global warming?

It is scare mongering! NOAA reported that almost all the allegedly "lost" ice has come back. The report reveals that ice levels which had shrunk from 5 million sq. miles in Jan. 2007 to just 1.5 million sq. miles in October 2007 are almost back to their original condition. The Feb. 18, 2008 *London Daily Express* report showed that there is nearly one third more ice in Antarctica than usual, **challenging global warming crusaders and buttressing arguments against global warming!**

If global warming gets any worse we'll all freeze to death!

Agenda

What is the environmental terrorist's agenda? The Green Movement is the new home of global socialism/communism. What the communists could not do through their military and political machinery they are now accomplishing through economic means. What they could not accomplish through brute force, they are now trying to accomplish by locking up the natural resources needed for biblically based capitalism to survive. As an example, they are against both pesticides and the use of biotechnology to increase crop yields, yet these things have tripled crop production since WW II.

Environmental terrorists are attempting to lock away natural resources, supposedly "preserving" them for the future with the noble goal of protecting animal and plant species and their habitat. But, this is actually an attempt to stop capitalism by removing the necessary resources for economic growth. Their main purpose is the abolition of personal property rights, which along with freedom of religion and speech, were primary reasons our forefathers founded the United States of America. Their final goal is the confiscation of all personal property because only the "government knows best," not "The Father knows best."

146

What Is the Difference Between Environmental Terrorist Preservation and Christian Conservation?

"Preservation" means to preserve a biological system exactly as it is "now" and to protect it from human intervention of any kind. An excellent example of this would be the legislation which brought the National Park Service into existence. The National Park system preserves unique land in its supposedly "pristine state" so that future generations may see these great natural wonders. The National Park system then builds as few roads and trails as possible in order to prevent people from seeing these great natural wonders.

The National Park's preservationist mentality proceeds to allow fires to burn out of control, thus destroying these great natural wonders given to their care, because fire is "natural." This happened in 1988 when the National Park system refused to stop relatively small fires which then enveloped Yellowstone National Park. Before the bureaucrats realized their error, they allowed 1,200,000 acres (1/3) of Yellowstone National Park to burn to the ground; costing $120 million to control; killing untold numbers of animals and plants; and destroying buildings worth $3 million.

How does one "preserve" a living system anyway? Is it possible or even desirable to "preserve" your baby as he/she was at, say, six months of age? The only way to "preserve" a living system, to keep it exactly the way it is at any given time, is to kill it and stick it in a bottle of formaldehyde! Living systems cannot be preserved; it is impossible! The preservation of certain trees today will never guarantee that those same trees will be seen by "our grandchildren."

Living systems, such as a forest, are dynamic, ever-changing entities. There is a specific life cycle which all forests experience. Bare ground (whether from fire or tree harvesting) is first covered by wild flowers and grasses. These are replaced by shrubs and fast growing conifers, like pines. Eventually, broadleaf hardwood trees, such as oak and hickory, will grow under the pines and will replace the pines. The hardwoods will continue to control the site until they die from old age. Once the hardwoods die off, the ground will once again be open and will be covered by grasses. This cycle will repeat itself as long as the world turns. It is God's plan. You cannot preserve a biological system and have it live at the same time. You may only manage a living system for "Someone" else.

Conservation

Christian Conservation means to work with a long term view and multiple goals for the wise use of natural resources; to prevent waste, to maximize benefit, to stress the wise use of renewable resources.

An excellent secular example of this would be the legislation which brought the National Forest Service into existence. The Forest Service manages the lands entrusted to it by the American people. The Forest Service plans for the multiple-use of all the resources which it controls; allowing for hunting, fishing, camping, tourism, wildlife management and sustained yield timber production. Anything which would destroy these resources is dealt with quickly, such as putting out forest fires.

You cannot preserve a biological system; you can kill it or you can conserve it. Conservation management by the Forest Service increases the total amount of wildlife and trees occupying the land, as well as their visibility and use by the public. The Forest Service attempts to exercise dominion and stewardship over the lands and resources entrusted to it.

What Should the Christian Position Be on Preservation Versus Conservation?

Preservation is an ungodly principle which promotes man-centered philosophies. No human is capable of perfectly planning ahead and foreseeing all the environmental consequences of his actions. No one may lock up biological systems and reasonably expect them to stay the way they were at the time of preservation.

"Christian Conservation" is the Godly use of all the natural resources that God has entrusted unto us. It is not locking away natural resources so that no one may use them as the unfaithful servant did. It is taking dominion and stewardship over that part of the creation which the Creator has given to each of us and giving it back to Him with an increase as our offering of thanksgiving for Who He is and what He means to us.

Christians should favor good stewardship of our God-given natural resources, and need not fear the destruction of our planet, as the non-believers do. We are told that there will be Christians here to greet Him when He returns!

For further information on this subject I would recommend reading the following:

- *Climate of Fear*, Thomas Gale Moore, Cato Institute, 1998.

- *Environmental Overkill: Whatever Happened to Common Sense?* Dr. Dixy Lee Ray, Regnery Gateway, 1993.

- *In a Dark Wood*, Alston Chase, Houghton Mifflin Co., 1995.

- *The Redwood National Park: A Case Study in Legislative Compromise*, Grady S. McMurtry, SUNY, Syracuse, NY, 1972

- *The True State of the Planet*, Ronald Bailey, Free Press, 1995.

- *The Skeptical Environmentalist: Measuring the Real State of the World*, Bjorn Lomborg, Cambridge University Press, 2001.

- *Hot Talk Cold Science: Global Warming's Unfinished Debate*, S. Fred Singer, The Independent Institute, 1998.

- *The Satanic Gases: Clearing the Air about Global Warming*, Patrick J. Michaels and Robert C. Billing, Jr., Cato Institute, 2000.

- *Global Warming and Other Eco-Myths*, edited by Ronald Bailey, Competitive Enterprise Institute, Prima Publishing, 2002.

- *Hard Green: Saving the Environment from the Environmentalists*, Peter Huber, Basic Books, Perseus Books Group, 1999.

- *Meltdown: The Predictable Distortion of Global Warming by Scientists, Politicians, and the Media*, Patrick J. Michaels, Cato Institute, 2004.

- *Challenging Environmental Mythology: Wrestling Zeus*, Jack W. Dini, Scitech Publishing, 2003.

- *The Politically Incorrect Guide to Global Warming and Environmentalism*, Christopher C. Horner, Regnery Publishing, 2007.

- *The Really Inconvenient Truths*, Iain Murray, Regnery Publishing, 2008.

- *Cool It*, Bjorn Lomborg, Knopf, 2007.

- *Unstoppable Global Warming: Every 1,500 Years*, Siegfried Fred Singer and Dennis T. Avery, Rowman & Littlefield, 2007.

THE COMPLEXITY OF THE UNIVERSE

The study of the creation from the most microscopic subatomic particle to the most macroscopic edge of the universe shows both the existence of God and the awesome magnificence of His creative powers. Some of the most basic questions of life are: How did I get here? What is my purpose? Do I accept the rules and the roles which God has given me? The Bible says that God is evident because of the unseen things which He has made. This chapter will delve into the unseen or little appreciated "things" of this universe which should, by their witness, press us into God our Creator and should make us realize that we do, indeed, have a purpose.

Let Us Look at the Complexity of Some "Simple" Mathematics

Mathematics is perhaps the only pure science. Two plus two equals four regardless of the other laws of science or the interpretations and bias of men.

Everything in the universe is intrinsically linked together. Some evolutionists say that there is a blind watchmaker who made the universe. The truth is that there is a Watchmaker Who is clearly seen because He made the watch. Let's use mathematics, probability, logic and the irreducible complexity contained in the universe to "see" the Watchmaker.

What Is the Probability of a Complex System Arising by Chance?

Start with the assumption that we have available a sea of freely available components capable of performing a specific useful function. Envision an organism made up out of only 100 parts (a truly simple organism), then only one combination of these parts would perform their function correctly. There are 100! (100 Factorial=100x99x98x97x...x1) or 10^{105} different combinations in which 100 parts may exist. So your chances of success in randomly picking out the one correct combination is 1 in 10^{105} (that is 1 chance in 1 followed by 158 zeros).

Now make some very conservative assumptions and see if it is possible to correctly pick out the one correct group of 100 from that sea of components by random chance. There are 10^{80} atoms in the entire known universe. If they were used to represent the useful components they could be grouped in groups of 100 (10^{2}) so there could only be 10^{80} minus 10^{2} or 10^{78} groups at any one time. If we assume that we have up to 30 billion years of time, could we find the one correct combination? There are 10^{18} seconds in 30 billion years. Make another assumption, that the groups of 100 components can combine, break apart and recombine at a billion times per second (10^{9} times per second) in order to make the one correct combination. Under such very generous conditions, what is the maximum number of combinations which could be made?

The answer is $10^{78} \times 10^{9} \times 10^{18} = 10^{105}$. The chance of one combination being correct is the total number of combinations needed to get one correct combination (10^{158}) minus the total number of combinations which can possibly be made under such generous conditions (10^{105}), or 10^{158} minus 10^{105} or one chance in 10^{53} (that is 1 chance in 1 followed by 53 zeros). That is no chance at all! Yet an organism of only 100 component parts is impossibly small. The simplest protein molecule has 400 linked amino acids and each amino acid has 4 to 5 chemical elements.

There are 206 bones in the human body, but there is only one correct combination in a human skeleton. To insure finding the one right combination of bones in all the possible combinations we would have to try 206! = 10^{375} different combinations.

The human brain has 10,000,000,000 (10^{10}) nerve cells in the cerebral cortex, all of which are arranged in a very orderly fashion. Consider the number of combinations in which they could be arranged in order to find the one correct combination (that's 10^{10} Factorial).

Some evolutionists have looked at similar statistics themselves and agreed that evolution on earth is an impossibility. Sir Fred Hoyle calculated the possibility of evolution having occurred on earth even one time and came to the conclusion that it would be equal to a tornado going through a junk yard and assembling a Boeing 747 ready to fly! The number of stars in the known universe is 10^{25}. The number of electrons (subatomic particles of which there must be at least one or more per atom, plus innumerable free ones) in the known universe is 10^{80}. The probability that a tornado could go through a junk yard and assemble a Boeing 747 ready to fly is 1 chance in $10^{40,000}$ attempts.

One of Sir Fred Hoyle's colleagues, the world class mathematician Chandra Wickramasinghe, made a similar calculation and came up with this example to explain the probability of evolution occurring even one time on earth. He said that it would be the same as a line of 50,000,000 blind men all solving a Rubik's cube at **exactly the same time!** When was the last time two blind men solved a Rubik's cube at exactly the same time?

What about the Size of the Universe?

How big is the earth? The earth is about 25,000 miles in circumference. The speed of sound is about 740 miles per hour. At the speed of sound, it would take 34 hours to go around the earth.

The moon is about 220,000+ miles from the earth. The spacecraft sent to the moon in the 1970's traveled at an average of 18,000 miles per hour or 300 miles per minute or 5 miles per second. At the same speed it would take 7.1 months to reach our sun.

The sun is about 92,000,000 miles from the earth. The speed of light is about 186,282 miles per second. It takes about eight minutes for light to travel from the sun to the earth. (Now please pick up a Bible and hold a single page of it between two of your fingers.)

How big is the Universe? Let the thickness of that Bible page equal the distance from the sun to the earth or 92,000,000 miles. At the speed of light it would take 100,000 years to go across our galaxy, the Milky Way. The distance across the Milky Way is equal to a stack of those Bible pages like the ones between your fingers **216 miles high!** The Milky Way is an ordinary sized galaxy consisting of about one billion stars and is only one galaxy among millions of other galaxies in the universe.

What about the Complexity of Biological Life Forms?

We start with the classic question, "Which came first, the chicken or the egg?" The DNA molecule carries the genetic information required for the construction of proteins and all other components of a living creature. The replication and transcription of DNA molecules require a complex set of enzymes and other proteins to be present. In other words, proteins are required for DNA synthesis, and DNA is required for protein synthesis. This makes chemical evolution an impossibility. We have then an irreducibly complex system. The obvious answer to the question above is that the fully grown chicken was required first in order to get the egg and care for the chick.

Biochemical machines like our bodies must have been designed by a higher intelligence, a God. When we look at the myriad of systems within our bodies, it becomes obvious that each is interrelated and interdependent upon each other. This makes life an irreducibly complex, finely-calibrated molecular mechanism. Each interacting component is indispensable for the functioning of all other components. If any one of these components is removed, the whole system may or will stop functioning.

Let us again use mathematics to get a concept of the complexity of life. A quark is considered to be the smallest known subatomic particle. Atoms are the smallest complete basic building blocks of all other structures in the universe. The smallest amino acid in a human cell consists of more than 4,000 atoms, each one of which must be in exactly the right place or it will not work. Proteins are made up of many amino acid chains, and proteins are an infinitesimally small part of a whole cell. You could put 70 human cells laid side by side across the width of the period at the end of this sentence.

What are the simplest cells capable of doing? Take the "simplest" E. coli bacteria, one with the least amount of DNA in it, one containing only a single strand of DNA. That "simple" cell can do 3,000 to 4,000 different chemical reactions, all at the same time and at the rate of one million times per second. Can you? The cells in your body are doing similar things all the time. That means that this "simple" cell is processing chemicals (information) three times faster than the fastest personal computer can process information.

What about the information **contained** inside one human cell? There is enough information in a single human cell containing complete genetic information (excluding blood and sex cells), that if it were printed out, it would fill 10,000 books the size of the *Encyclopedia Britannica*. There is enough DNA information contained in the cells of one average human being to print enough books to fill the Grand Canyon of Arizona 40 times! The Grand Canyon is up to 1.2 miles deep, varies from 0.1 miles to 18 miles wide, and is 277 miles long. That information is equal to 5×10^{15} (5 zillion) books or one billion times the number of books contained in the Library of Congress. That amount of information is equal to one million times more books than are contained in the world's 1,000 largest libraries.

What about the Complexity of the Human Body?

The Greek writer, Sophocles, once wrote, "Numberless are the world's wonders, but none are more wonderful than man, himself." Sophocles's timeless words still ring true today, for human life continues to exist as the crowning achievement of God's creation. Consider the unimaginable complexity and potential of the human brain, the architectural masterwork of the hand and skeletal system, and the incredible durability of the human heart. Contained within the human body, God's creative power expresses its magnificent dimensions. But, there is far more to the miracle of the human experience than the wonders of the body and the mind. God has made each one of us for a specific purpose; and He has made each one of us for the highest purpose of all, to know and enjoy His love and care for us, forever.

Let's look at just what is inside an "average" human cell. Human cells vary in size from 1/100th of a millimeter long to two meters long. There are about 30 trillion cells in an "average" human body, each of which may perform up to 10,000 different chemical functions within it. Each cell, with its complete genetic information, has one trillion (10^{12}) bits of data contained on its DNA molecules which is equal to 100,000 coded messages. One trillion bits of information is equivalent to every letter printed inside 10,000,000 average-sized books. The average life expectancy of a human cell is seven years, during which time it leads an independent life but cooperates with millions of other cells. The chromosomes in each cell are made up of 200 million nucleotides, which contain the information as described above.

How about the nervous system? There are more than 3 trillion nerve cells controlling body functions. If they were to be lined up end-to-end they would extend for 45 miles. There are 120 trillion "connections" between all these cells. By comparison, a bee has only 900 nerve cells, and an ant only 250. Human nerve impulses move at about 300 miles per hour. Our internal information network processes 100 million electro-chemical impulses per second, yet the whole system weighs less than 2% of our total body weight. Each day our brains process more than 10,000 thoughts and concepts. Isn't that simple?

What about the human voice? The human voice can be reliably heard from as far away as 600 feet away. The whistling language of "Silbo," used in the Canary Islands, may be heard up to six miles away. The English language contains more than 500,000 basic words, while the normal person has a vocabulary of only 50,000 words. The use of human "Body Language" may convey an additional four to eight thousand thoughts.

What about human eyesight? Vision accounts for 90 to 95% of all our sensory perception. The eye is a fully automatic, self-focusing, non-blurring, color motion-picture camera which takes instant high-resolution photos. On a moonless night, a person sitting on a mountain top may see the light of a match from 50 miles away. The eye has more than 120 million photo-receptors which can perceive more than one million simultaneous impressions. It can discriminate between nearly 10 million color varieties. So much for black and white.

How about our hearing? The human ear has 24,000 "hair cells" which convert sound vibrations into electrical impulses. We can discriminate among more than 300,000 tones. Our ears are remarkably sensitive, being able to pick up sound waves with as little power as 10^{-16} of a watt. (If they were only slightly more sensitive, we would actually be able to hear air molecules striking our eardrums.) The human ear can endure short-lived surges of sound more than 100 million times higher than its minimum level. This is about the same as the energy output of a small city. If it were not for the fact that our eardrums were only about one square centimeter, we would all be deaf. The ear also has an automatic built-in volume control. Aren't you glad?

How about our noses? They are so sensitive that they are able to smell concentrations of some chemicals down to only one part in 32 billion parts of air. At the same time our noses are smelling, they also clean, warm and humidify more than 500 cubic feet of air each day.

How about our 35 foot long alimentary canal? We only require three and a half pounds of food each day to be well nourished. Our food is chewed by 32 teeth and mixed with saliva, which is a mild digestive substance, produced by the five salivary glands located in our mouths. The normal person swallows about 2,000 times per day. The stomach is lined with 35 million digestive glands to digest food, but must be able to not digest itself. The acid in your stomach is strong enough to dissolve varnish. The small intestine is about 20 feet long and breaks up what we eat into vitamins, minerals and food which must be able to be absorbed into the bloodstream through tissue walls. Because of its folds and projections, the small intestine has a surface area of 2 million square inches or about equal to the size of a tennis court.

How about the heart and blood? If all the blood vessels in a human body were stretched from end-to-end, they would encircle the earth. The blood supply contains 180 trillion red blood cells, 30 million white corpuscles and trillions of other blood cells. The heart moves a volume of about 2,000 gallons of blood each day. In an average lifetime, the heart will pump from 800,000 to 1.6 million gallons of blood through it which is enough to fill two hundred 8,000 gallon railroad tank cars. The body contains 100,000 miles of blood vessels. The heart beats an average of 100,000 times per day, a total of 2.5 billion times in 72 years. During an 80-year-lifetime, blood would flow a total distance of 168 million miles. In order to replace the used up red blood cells, the bone marrow produces 70,000 new cells per minute, a total of a billion a day. The kidneys contain more than 40 miles of cleansing filters and clean more than 500 gallons of blood per day. One quarter of the entire blood supply flows through the kidneys every minute.

How about the lungs? On average, we take 23,800 breaths per day, for a total of about 438 cubic feet of air. The air passages in our nose, throat and lungs filter the air with a sticky mucous film. The lungs contain more than 750 million air sacs, or *alveoli,* which if they were opened up and spread out flat, would total 1,000 square feet.

How about the liver? The liver performs more than 500 functions and makes more than 1,000 different enzymes. It is a veritable living chemical plant. It breaks down harmful compounds and makes essential chemicals all at the same time.

How about the skin? The body is cooled by approximately 2 million sweat glands which keep the temperature correct to within one degree. The skin has about 4 million sensory cells of one kind or another and contains about 500,000 touch sensors. But, for those who enjoy sitting out in the sun, it has only 200,000 temperature sensors. The skin contains oil glands which keep the skin from drying out and keeps it flexible. The skin is the largest organ in the body.

How about the rest of the body? The body contains 206 bones and 639 muscles. If all the muscles in the body were to pull together in one direction they would be able to lift more than 25 tons off the ground! Each step we take requires the instantaneous coordination of about 300 muscles. The 206 bones in a body weigh only about 20 pounds. The average person flexes their finger joints more than 25 million times during their lifetime. The human brain is still capable of outperforming the fastest of the super-fast Super Computers. Will man ever design a computer better than the human brain? No! No one can create anything that is greater than himself.

How Valuable Is This Complexity?

How valuable is an irreducibly complex human life? Please read Ephesians 2:10. It says that we are all His workmanship. Well, who is the He? He is God and He is perfect. When He makes something it will at least start out perfect. Therefore Ephesians 2:10 actually says in the Greek language, "For we are His **masterpiece**." What is a masterpiece? It is the greatest single work of art produced by a particular master-artist. An example would be Leonardo da Vinci's *Mona Lisa*.

What **does** it take to produce a masterpiece? First, it takes the skill of the master; no novice may paint a masterpiece. Then there is the plan of the master. No master-painter would start to paint a landscape and end up with a portrait. Would he simply pick up the very next canvas or wouldn't he sort through a hundred canvases until he found a perfect canvas? Next, he would hand-select the colors and hand-apply them to the canvas. There is even a scientific method of how to tell one master from another, merely based upon the individual painter's brush stroke technique. In Psalm 139, it says that we were embroidered in our mother's womb. Anyone may weave burlap, but only a master may weave embroidery.

Once a masterpiece is finished, would you ever take anything away or add anything to it? Never. Once finished, wouldn't a frame which accentuates the painting perfectly be purchased? But, the frame also sets the limits of the picture, doesn't it? The frame says that everything inside the frame is picture and everything outside the frame is not.

This is what God did. He has a purpose and plan for each of us. He chose the color of our eyes, the color of our hair and the color of our skin and He hand applied them to the canvas that is us. When He was finished, He put a frame around us and said that we were complete.

What is the value of a masterpiece? Would the French ever sell the *Mona Lisa*? Would the Pope ever sell the ceiling of the Sistine Chapel? They are not for sale at any price. What then is the value of a masterpiece? It is **priceless!**

This is why God is the only One in the whole universe Who had something worth trading for you, a priceless masterpiece; and that is when He sent His only Son to die on a cross for you to pay the purchase price, the redemption price, the exchange price for you, His priceless masterpiece.

If you have ever had a problem with self-esteem, personal value or personal worth, perhaps you should look again; take these comments and change your mind about how valuable you are in God's sight. He exchanged the only thing in the universe worth the price of a priceless masterpiece for you. If that is His opinion, why should you think anything less of yourself?

OTHER REFERENCE SOURCES

Austin, Steven. *Catastrophes in Earth History*. Inst. for Creation Research, El Cajon, CA, 1984.

Austin, Steven. *Grand Canyon: Monument to Catastrophe*. Inst. For Creation Research, Santee, CA. 1994.

Bliss, Richard, and Gary Parker. *Origin of Life*. Master Books, Green Forest, AR, 1979.

Brown, Walter. *In the Beginning*. Center for Scientific Creation, Phoenix, 1996.

Davis, Percival, and Dean Kenyon. *Of Pandas and People*. Haughton Pub. Co., Dallas, 1989.

Denton, Michael. *Evolution: A Theory in Crisis*. Burnett Books Ltd., London, 1985.

Denton, Michael. *Nature's Destiny*. The Free Press, New York, NY, 1998.

Fields, Weston. *Unformed and Unfilled: A Critique of the Gap Theory*. Burgener Ent., Collinsville, IL, 1994.

Gentry, Robert. *Creation's Tiny Mystery*. Earth Science Associates, 1986.

Gish, Duane. *Evolution: Challenge of the Fossil Record*. Master Books, Green Forest, AR, 1976.

Ham, Ken, Andrew Snelling, and Carl Wieland. *The Answers Book*. Master Books, Green Forest, AR, 1992.

Johnson, Phillip. *Darwin on Trial*. InterVarsity Press, Downers Grove, IL, 1993.

Lubenow, Marvin. *Bones of Contention*. Baker Book House, Grand Rapids, 1992.

Morris, Henry. *The Biblical Basis for Modern Science*. Baker Book House, Grand Rapids, 1986.

Morris, Henry, and John Morris. *The Modern Creation Trilogy*. Master Books, Green Forest, AR, 1996.

Morris, Henry, and John Whitcomb. *The Genesis Flood*. Pres. and Ref. Pub. Co., Phila., 1961.

Morris, Henry. *The Genesis Record*. Baker Book House, Grand Rapids, 1976.

Morris, Henry. *The Long War against God*. Baker Book House, Grand Rapids, 1989.

Morris, Henry. *Men of Science/Men of God*. Master Books, Green Forest, AR, 1988.

Morris, Henry. *The Remarkable Record of Job*. Baker Book House, Grand Rapids, 1988.

Morris, Henry. *Scientific Creationism*. Master Books, Green Forest, AR, 1985.

Morris, Henry. *That Their Words May Be Used Against Them*. Master Books, Green Forest, AR, 1997.

Morris, Henry, and Gary Parker. *What Is Creation Science?* Master Books, Green Forest, AR, 1987.

Morris, John. *The Young Earth*. Master Books, Green Forest, AR, 1994.

Noebel, David. *Understanding the Times*. Harvest House Publishers, Eugene, Oregon, 1991.

Peterson, Dennis. *Unlocking the Mysteries of Creation*. Creation Resource Foundation, El Dorado, CA, 1986.

Sunderland, Luther. *Darwin's Enigma: Fossils and Other Problems*: Master Books, Colorado Springs, 1998.

Taylor, Ian. *In the Minds of Men*. TFE Publishing, Toronto, 1987.

Thaxton, Charles, Walter Bradley, and Roger Olsen. *The Mystery of Life's Origin: Reassessing Current Theories*. New York: Philosophical Library, 1984.

Whitcomb, John. *The World That Perished*. Baker Book House, Grand Rapids, 1994.